A Different Kind of Laughter

A Different Kind of Laughter

Finding Joy and Peace in the Deep End of Life

Andy Cook

Kregel
Publications

A Different Kind of Laughter: Finding Joy and Peace in the Deep End of Life

© 2002 by Andy Cook

Published by Kregel Publications, a division of Kregel, Inc., P.O. Box 2607, Grand Rapids, MI 49501. For more information about Kregel Publications, visit our Web site: www.kregel.com.

Cover design: John M. Lucas

ISBN 0-8254-2387-2

Printed in the United States of America

02 03 04 05 / 5 4 3 2 1

*This book is dedicated
to the ever-laughing believers who are
Shirley Hills Baptist Church.*

To God be the glory.

Contents

He Always Had It in Him

E ven as a three-year-old, Andy Cook had it in him to be a preacher.

Back then, however, he sometimes confused his Bible verses with his nursery rhymes. He would stand on top of his toy box and deliver a sermon to his family: "And Moses said . . . the mouse ran up the clock!"

Years later, when he had sorted out the differences between the Ten Commandments and "Hickory, Dickory, Dock," he held a deep belief that the ministry would one day be his calling.

It didn't happen right away. God steered Andy around some sharp curves and pushed him up some steep hills before finally directing him to the pulpit.

I'm glad there was a slight delay; otherwise, our paths might never have crossed.

I first met Andy in 1980 when he joined the sports department of the *Macon Telegraph and News*. We not only became colleagues, we also became fast friends.

For the next eight years we worked side by side. We wrote stories together. We laid out pages together. We raced toward deadline together. We pulled our hair together. I'm proud to say that our friendship has entered its twentieth year.

I guess what attracted us and cemented our friendship were the common denominators. We were in love with the same things.

Georgia football.

Playing the guitar.

Creative writing.

The sound of our hearts when we stood over a four-foot birdie putt. (Or any birdie putt, for that matter.)

We both loved the Lord, too.

Oh, there were a few differences. Andy hates tomatoes with a passion. Can hardly stand to be in the same room with them. Give me a couple of homegrown 'maters on white bread, slap on some mayonnaise, salt, and pepper, and I'll be happy for life.

Andy and his wife, Melody, have been blessed with three beautiful daughters. On the other hand, my wife, Delinda, and I have been blessed with three handsome sons. So Andy knows a lot more about girl stuff than I do.

I remember when Andy told me he had decided to leave the newspaper business and enter the seminary. We were in the car late one night, driving back from a game we had covered.

He said he was trading in the Bulldogs and Braves for the Bible and the Beatitudes. I can't say that I was surprised. After all, he always had it in him to be a preacher.

But the years wandering in the wilderness—four years of college and eight years as a sports writer—weren't wasted. Those years helped prepare him for his current role in life.

Friends come into and go out of your life like the changing seasons. I'm grateful that Andy and I have remained close. We love each other like brothers. We've known each other for roughly half our lives.

I'm thankful that, when he departed for a seminary in Wake Forest, North Carolina, we stayed in touch during those years. A letter. A phone call. A prayer.

I was there at his ordination at the Bellevue Baptist Church in Macon, his home church. I visited with him when he pastored a small church in Castalia, North Carolina. I heard him preach on a sweltering Sunday morning at the First Baptist Church of Soperton. The place was so jam-packed to hear "Brother Andy" that the only things that outnumbered the congregation were the south Georgia gnats.

Since he became pastor of Shirley Hills Baptist in Warner Robins in 1997, I've watched Andy do remarkable things. He not only has energized a church but he's also led a community. I'm sure that he's made front-row Baptists out of a lot of folks—and that's not always easy to do.

He has loved. He has comforted. He has inspired. And that's what he does with the words in this book.

As you read, you will find peace.

As you read, you will gain a better understanding of the love of Jesus, who saved some of his best teaching for last.

And, as you read, you will understand why I value Andy's friendship so much.

Yep. He always had it in him to be a preacher.

—ED GRISAMORE
columnist, *Macon Telegraph*

A cheerful disposition is good for your health; gloom and doom leave you bone-tired.

—Proverbs 17:22 *(The Message)*

One

Desperately Needing the Laughter

In a season of dryness, I went on a search for the laughter. I was physically, emotionally, and spiritually tired. I longed for the laughter that I had known as a child, when I had laughed enough to create the permanent creases in my face today.

Life can steal your laughter in a hurry—with a crisis, with the daily grind. Throw in a few personal struggles, a major disappointment or two, and you'll wonder where the smiles went.

Every Sunday, I tell anyone who'll listen that the answers are in the Bible. No matter what the question, the answer is there.

In my own search for laughter, I hoped I could find the answer. My journey through Scripture started in predictable places. I camped out in Philippians—the "Joy Book" of the Bible—and I hiked through the Psalms. I hunted for joy, peace, and laughter, and I almost gave up. I didn't doubt the Scripture, but I was beginning to worry about myself. I missed the laughter, and I hated what stress was doing to me.

Do you remember the stories of America's Gold Rush in 1849? Much of America caught "gold fever" and headed for the mines in California. Most of the stories of that time deal with the crowds that pushed West, but recently I've thought about the fellow who stumbled across that first golden nugget. Maybe he was scooping a drink of water from a stream when a glimmer caught his eye. Then perhaps he saw another glimmer. He surely wasn't expecting a miracle. But he took time to reach for the gold that had been waiting for him, and his life was changed. And thousands of other lives were changed, too.

My experience was something like that. I wasn't expecting to find laughter where I found it. It never occurred to me that there would be any joy in the Upper Room or any laughter coming from the cross. But maybe I had been looking for the wrong kind of laughter. What I found was a different kind of laughter. This laughter was more meaningful, deeper, and more satisfying than any I had found before, far beyond the chuckle of a good joke or the temporary smile after a perfect day. No, this was much better. This kind of laughter is more valuable than that prospector's gold in California. Just as his nugget sparkled in spring water, the golden nuggets from the last teaching of Christ had been gleaming from Scripture all my life. I picked up first one nugget and then another.

The gold rush was on.

The intensity of the last few hours of Jesus' teaching, which we're about to cover in this book, is unmatched. Before that night was over, he had been painfully straightforward with his disciples; his brow had broken into a bloody sweat because of his distress. It doesn't look like a time for laughter. But listen closely to what Jesus says during those powerful moments. Here, Jesus tells us repeatedly that we can have lives filled with joy, peace, and blessings. He practically begs us to enjoy life to its fullest and to tap into the abundant life made available by the cross. Some of the truth was new to me, and some of it simply reminded me of truths I already knew.

Before we begin, a word of warning and a quick illustration. If you're looking for your laughter, the instruction from Jesus will give it to you. Make no mistake about it. You *will* find the formula for finding it in what the Lord said. Applying his instruction, however, might be one of the most difficult things you've ever done. I struggle with some of the instruction every day, and I struggled mightily with it as I put these words together. I suppose that I shall struggle with it for the rest of my life.

Then again, finding the laughter isn't nearly as hard as we make it out to be. I remember from my childhood a number of incidents that should have been troubling to me. Maybe I spilled the milk, dropped a potted plant, or generally made a mess of something. My mom, the eternal optimist, had a little saying: "Well, you can cry if you want, but crying won't help. So you know what? You might as well laugh."

That's still a good idea. As I studied the last teaching of Christ, I found my laughter again. I offer a prayer that you, too, will find the very joy, peace, and blessings that Jesus promised. Of all the options available in life, there's a simple one you could choose, and I hope you do: You might as well laugh!

Two

Three Promises

L ate in the summer of 1980, my wife and I were in the backyard of Georgia football coach Vince Dooley and his talkative
wife, Barbara. Dooley was the coach of the Bulldogs, and
Barbara—among other things—hawked hot dogs. She appeared
often on television, selling "Dooley's other dogs." So at the picnic
we made small talk while an amazing variety of "Dooley's other
dogs" turned bronze on the grill.

I was a college student/sports writer, one of several local writers who was enjoying a preseason visit that day to the coach's
home. The Dooleys didn't know us very well, so the subject of
conversation obviously fell to my wife's stomach. Melody was—
we were—expecting a baby. By now, on the verge of autumn, she
was *obviously* expecting.

"When are you due?" Barbara asked Melody.

"In late October," Melody said, trying to fit a humongous hot
dog into a bun.

"Oh good," said the coach's wife, who immediately associated the date of birth with the date of the Georgia-Vanderbilt game. "You can name it *Vandy* if it's a boy, or *Victoria* if it's a girl—because you know we'll win that game!"

Vanderbilt was something of an annual pushover in those days for Dooley's Dogs, but the coach was superstitious. He had veteran quarterback Buck Belue for that 1980 season, and he might even have been secretly optimistic that freshman recruit Herschel Walker might make a difference. But the coach would not jinx himself out of a win over Vandy. So he steered away from any suggestion that Vanderbilt was an easy win.

"No, no," Dooley said. "You can name it Buck."

"Coach," I asked, "what if it's a girl?"

"Well," he grinned, "you can call her *Her-SHELL.*"

We all smiled, and Melody and I moved on down the chow line. Later on, in the car on the way home, I caught the glare in Melody's eyes. Through her clenched teeth she snarled, "We will not, under any circumstances, name this baby for any football player."

I laughed at the very thought, agreed to forego *Her-SHELL,* and headed for home.

Two weeks after the Bulldogs' victory over Vanderbilt, our little girl came screaming, very overdue, into the world. We named her Summer Elaine just because we liked the sound of it. By the time we took her home, the whole town was in a football frenzy— Dooley's Bulldogs were ranked No. 1 in the nation and had only Auburn to beat the next week to win the Southeastern Conference title—the coveted SEC crown.

We walked toward our apartment in married housing, then froze in our tracks. Our neighbors, all college students, had taped a door-length "Welcome Home" banner to the front entrance.

Welcome Home,
Summer
Elaine
Cook!

Each letter of our child's initials was outlined in red and black, Georgia's school colors.

"S.E.C."

"Sweetheart, I can't believe it," I said. "You named her for the whole team!"

If we had known that Georgia would go on to win the national title that year, I suppose we'd have named our daughter *Dooley*.

My wife and I laugh when we talk about waiting for that first child. People told us how our lives were about to change, but we had no idea how much. We knew, intellectually, that a child was about to join us, but we simply couldn't comprehend it. I was almost shocked when I saw fingers and toes on this brand-new child. For nine months, we had lived with the *promise*. Now, for the last two decades, we've lived with the reality. She's in college as I write these words, and the shock of fingers and toes has worn off for the shock of seeing a young woman where a little girl used to be.

Take it from a father: On the pregnant side of a promise, it's impossible to comprehend the reality of the next twenty years. And in the same way, if you've never taken the promises of Jesus personally, you'll have a tough time comprehending the joy that's just ahead. First, of course, you must make the choice to rejoice.

The place we're about to go, however, doesn't look very joyful. It doesn't sound very joyful. Instead of laughter, we hear worried whispers and even a few complaints. Charges are made—and denied. A traitor will soon leave, anxious to hold his blood money. It smells in the room, for no one was willing to wash his own feet.

So Jesus took care of that by washing both his feet and theirs. In all, twenty-six feet with 130 muddy, callused toes . . . give or take a fishing accident or two.

Within hours, Jesus will be nailed to a cross. He alone is aware of his fate. His intensity is unmatched because he has only a few hours left to teach these men—these followers, these disciples—what he wants them to know. Jesus is about to give them three important promises that will change their lives. They could change your life, too.

Here's a quick overview. First, just after he puts up the dirty towels, he announces that he's about to teach. And up front he says, "Now that you know these things, *you will be blessed if you do them*" (John 13:17).

The promise of blessings. That's the first promise, and the first time one of the three promises is mentioned.

The second promise is given not once but twice in short order: "I have told you this so that my joy may be in you and that *your joy may be complete*" (John 15:11); "Until now you have not asked for anything in my name. Ask and you will receive, and *your joy will be complete*" (John 16:24).

The promise of complete joy. That's the second promise.

Near the end of the teaching, as the disciples (minus, of course, Judas Iscariot) reach the Garden of Gethsemane, Jesus sums up: "I have told you these things, so that *in me you may have peace*. In this world you will have trouble. But take heart! I have overcome the world" (John 16:33).

The promise of peace. That's the third promise.

Blessings. Joy. Peace.

These promises are akin to having triplets. If one baby changes a home, three turn it upside down! Here's a plainspoken triple promise from the Son of God: You can have his blessings, a "complete" joy, and an indescribable peace. These promises delineate what Jesus had already promised his followers: "I am come that they might have life, and that they might have it more abundantly" (John 10:10 KJV).

This teaching of Jesus is all the more profound because it's the last he will give before he dies. It was so intense, so powerful, that the disciple John was intent on every word. Jesus' words in the Upper Room and on the path to Gethsemane almost fill four complete chapters. If your Bible prints the words of Jesus in red ink, those chapters are awash in red.

And if you print those words on your heart, you'll be awash in joy. In fact, you'll have blessings, complete joy, and peace. They are three gifts that can bring laughter to your soul—not the shallow laughter that comes after a joke, but a deep laughter that keeps you going forward even if you're walking toward a cross. It's a different kind of laughter, one that is priceless to the soul.

If you're interested in the laughter, it's worth a return trip to the room where Jesus held audience with twelve men and their dirty feet.

Three

For Believers Only

The weight of Jesus' last teaching is especially heavy because of the timing. Jesus frames the last teaching of his life with three promises that we all desire—blessings, joy, and peace—promises that spell out the "abundant life" that Jesus offered in John 10:10.

But, again, think of Jesus' situation. Only he knows how quickly the end is coming. By the next morning, he'll be on a cross, laying down his life for the sins of the world. But earlier, he and the disciples meet in a private room and there experience what we call the Lord's Supper. The teaching begins here and continues as Jesus walks with the disciples to a place outside the city. Eventually, they make their way to the Garden of Gethsemane, where Judas becomes the most notorious traitor of all time. Before the betrayal, Jesus finishes this very serious teaching and prays so hard that, Dr. Luke tells us, he sweat droplets of blood from his forehead.

In the midst of all of that stress, Jesus talks about joy. He talks about heaven, and peace, and an ability to be blessed even in the middle of tough circumstances.

Before we hear all that Jesus said that night, however, we should look at a preliminary event that colors the entire evening.

Simply put, Judas left.

I used to feel sorry for Judas, but the more I study Scripture, the clearer picture I get of what actually happened.

Judas was with Jesus for three years. Judas was more familiar with Jesus than a Sunday regular in a favorite pew. He heard all of Jesus' words, saw all of the miracles, and even touched the supernatural. And by his own choice, on the last night of Jesus' life, he left.

The leaving was a long time in the making. After some three years of ministry, Jesus' work on earth was coming to an end. Jesus was taking dead aim on a cross that would mark the central point of all time. At the same time, Judas Iscariot, the one plainly identified as a betrayer by all four writers of the Gospels, was taking dead aim on his exit. From the day he began stealing from the disciples' moneybag (John 12:6), Judas was a traitor in the inner circle.

Matthew was there. Here's his account.

> Then one of the Twelve—the one called Judas Iscariot—went to the chief priests and asked, "What are you willing to give me if I hand him over to you?" So they counted out for him thirty silver coins. From then on Judas watched for an opportunity to hand him over.
>
> —Matthew 26:14–16

> While he was still speaking, Judas, one of the Twelve, arrived. With him was a large crowd armed with swords and clubs, sent from the chief priests and the elders of the people. Now the betrayer had arranged a signal with them: "The one I

kiss is the man; arrest him." Going at once to Jesus, Judas
said, "Greetings, Rabbi!" and kissed him.

—Matthew 26:47–49

There's no mistaking the intentional betrayal by Judas. We want
to think better of him. We want to consider him some kind of
demon-possessed victim who had no control over his actions.
But in the pages of Scripture, we see that Judas went to the chief
priests—and not the other way around. From the first, Judas asked
for money for his betrayal. Then Judas looked for the right time
and the right place to complete the deal. Judas also left the Upper Room on his own, and on his own led the soldiers across the
Kidron Valley to the base of the Mount of Olives, into Gethsemane,
the shady retreat he knew to be the favorite praying place for the
man he once thought to be the Messiah. Judas—no one else—
arranged for a signal to the soldiers. When they arrived, Judas
wasted no time, going *at once* to Jesus and giving the signal.

Before the actual betrayal, Judas was with Jesus in the Upper
Room. The disciples were there to celebrate the Passover meal,
usually one of the most joyful occasions of the year. At this particular meal, however, the joy and the passion were absent. It's
easy to imagine the state of the disciples. They must have been
cranky, sweaty, and frightened. The previous Sunday they had
been hailed as heroes. Now they were hiding. The shadows of
crosses hung over the entire group.

Judas sensed the opportunity to make his move. John sensed
that something was wrong. Peter was characteristically loud. A
nervous tension hung over the room.

Jesus took over. With a towel, a basin, and some water, he fo-
cused the group. He washed Peter's feet. He washed the feet of
Matthew, James, John, Thaddaeus, Andrew, Judas the son of
James, Philip, Bartholomew, James the son of Alphaeus, and
Simon the Zealot.

And Jesus washed the feet of Judas Iscariot. Jesus washed the feet of the person who would soon walk into the temple and collect a paycheck for murder. Jesus gently dried the ankles of the man who would forever defame one of the most common names in Israel. *Judas* was a good name. Jesus had a half-brother named Judas. By the time that Judas wrote a book of the Bible that bears his name, he had changed his name to Jude. Another disciple named Judas would always need a clarification in Scripture—"not *that* Judas."

Jesus finished washing feet, then started his last few hours of impassioned teaching. At the meal, according to John's record (John 13:23), Jesus sat next to John. In short order, Jesus announced that a betrayer was in the room. A cry of protest immediately arose. The disciples all cried out. Judas, too, expressed his objection, yet he knew his plan had already been set in motion. Then comes a revealing exchange. Simon Peter asked John to ask Jesus which disciple was the culprit. John, sitting next to Jesus, leaned back and asked for a clarification.

> Jesus answered, "It is the one to whom I will give this piece of bread when I have dipped it in the dish." Then, dipping the piece of bread, he gave it to Judas Iscariot, son of Simon. As soon as Judas took the bread, Satan entered into him.
>
> "What you are about to do, do quickly," Jesus told him, but no one at the meal understood why Jesus said this to him. Since Judas had charge of the money, some thought Jesus was telling him to buy what was needed for the Feast, or to give something to the poor. As soon as Judas had taken the bread, he went out. And it was night.
>
> —John 13:26–30

The record, then, reveals that John was sitting on one side of Jesus, and we know that Simon Peter was sitting on the other side of John. But we don't have a seating chart for the rest of the men. Jesus, however, is able to speak quietly to John and to speak softly to Judas. Only John was close enough to hear Jesus' words. Simon the Zealot, the one with the ready dagger, wasn't aware that Judas needed to have his throat cut. Peter, the rash one, didn't tackle the betrayer. Judas simply got up and exited into the darkness.

Do you comprehend what that softly spoken exchange means? Jesus had intentionally taken a place at this last meal next to Judas! Jesus hadn't given up on reaching Judas. Although many people have pictured Jesus holding out a *rope* to Judas, in reality, Jesus held out *hope*. He gave Judas one last opportunity for repentance at the last meal. But Judas would not accept that forgiveness. He was so sure that his way was better than *the*Way that he charged ahead with a bull-headed stubbornness. Granted, the Scripture says that "Satan entered into him," but never forget that Judas first opened the door to Satan.

A few hours later, Judas saw his plan falling apart. Did he comprehend that Jesus was about to die for him, Judas Iscariot?

There was one last critical moment when Judas was ripe for salvation.

> When Judas, who had betrayed him, saw that Jesus was condemned, he was seized with remorse and returned the thirty silver coins to the chief priests and the elders. "I have sinned," he said, "for I have betrayed innocent blood."
>
> "What is that to us?" they replied. "That's your responsibility."
>
> So Judas threw the money into the temple and left. Then he went away and hanged himself.
>
> —Matthew 27:3–5

Judas ran from the temple and out through the city gates. By his own choice and under his own power, Judas left.

Think about that. Judas ran out of the city in desperation. If he had gone in one direction, he would have seen the Son of God dying for his sins. Judas could have flung himself at the foot of the cross and asked for mercy. And he would have received it. But the tragedy is that Judas turned the other way, ran away from hope, and took for himself hopelessness instead.

But what happened in the Upper Room after Judas left? The other disciples stayed and received what might be the most profound teaching Jesus ever gave. And therein is the point: the teaching didn't begin until the betrayer was out of the room. John's gospel says, *"When [Judas] was gone,* Jesus said, *'Now* is the Son of Man glorified and God is glorified in him'" (John 13:31).

The teaching that followed on that momentous night would be for believers only. Yes, there is a "complete joy" that is promised by Jesus, but it's still only for those who have crossed over the line into faith, into a saving knowledge of Christ.

The teaching that follows in this book is also for believers only. This is not a self-help book for the world. And neither will this book make sense to those who are wavering in their faith. Rather, this book offers insight for those who already have made the step of faith to stay in the room with Jesus, no matter what the future holds. If you've made that commitment, listen to the teaching as if you were in the very room. The formula for joy is just moments away.

Four

The Lesson of Love

Comedienne Rita Rudner must have been cooking when she made this observation: "If you put flour and water together, you have glue. If you add butter and eggs, you have the makings of a cake. So where did the glue go?"

The disciples had walked with Jesus for the better part of three years. They were growing in faith. They were doing a lot of good things. But up to this point, their mixture of faith and good works were a little like mixing flour and water. Until they learned to add love and forgiveness, they'd be missing part of the recipe—and would likely end up with only a sticky mess.

There was certainly a mess in the Upper Room the night before Jesus died. Twelve men entered that room with Jesus, and all twelve were capable of washing feet. They could have washed their own feet, but they didn't. Perhaps it was haste, or irritability, or most likely pride that caused them to skip the habit their mothers had taught them decades before. Whatever the reason, they reclined, grumpy before their holiday meal, each of them getting his feet too close to the food, too close to someone else's nose.

They were so self-centered, they didn't even notice when Jesus headed for the towel closet. When he returned, Jesus had stripped down and wrapped himself in the towel he would need for the task. He carried a bowl of water in his hands and an object lesson in his actions.

Washing the disciples' feet was such a powerful demonstration that none of them could speak. Peter protested for a moment but then accepted the gift. The room fell silent and serious, each man kicking himself for not doing what should have already been done.

John was so moved that his mind became sharper than it had ever been. What Jesus would say to the group on this night, John would later write down for us, word for word.

It didn't take long for Jesus to drive home the object lesson: It wasn't that important, he said, simply to keep good hygiene around the table; it was important to find a way to love other people. It was important to shift the focus from self to others, to make servanthood a natural way of living.

After the meal, it was time to expound on the lesson. Jesus exposed the betrayer, even though only he and Judas were aware of the deceit in the room. When Judas left—with clean feet, no less—Jesus was ready to teach.

> When [Judas] *was gone,* Jesus said, "Now is the Son of Man glorified and God is glorified in him. If God is glorified in him, God will glorify the Son in himself, and will glorify him at once.
>
> "My children, I will be with you only a little longer. You will look for me, and just as I told the Jews, so I tell you now: Where I am going, you cannot come.

"A new command I give you: Love one another. As I have loved you, so you must love one another. By this all men will know that you are my disciples, if you love one another."

—John 13:31–35

If you're looking for the blessings, joy, and peace that Jesus offers, listen closely to the instructions. They're not hard to comprehend. They're as plainly spoken as possible: "A new command I give you: Love one another."

Need some clarification on the command? Jesus says, "As I have loved you, so you must love one another."

Need a word picture that demonstrates the command? Look at Jesus after the foot washing, making his embarrassed men look him in the eye. His hands are filthy, he's sweating in the springtime heat, and he himself needs to get cleaned up. But no condemnation proceeds from Jesus. In a few moments, however, he returns to the room with the words that the disciples are finally ready to hear.

> When he had finished washing their feet, he put on his clothes and returned to his place. "Do you understand what I have done for you?" he asked them. "You call me 'Teacher' and 'Lord,' and rightly so, for that is what I am. Now that I, your Lord and Teacher, have washed your feet, you also should wash one another's feet. I have set you an example that you should do as I have done for you. I tell you the truth, no servant is greater than his master, nor is a messenger greater than the one who sent him. Now that you know these things, *you will be blessed if you do them.*"
>
> —John 13:12–17

Need another word picture for the kind of love Jesus was talking about? By the next afternoon, they would see how far Jesus would take his love for them. But he would first spell it out after the foot washing: "Greater love has no one than this, that he lay down his life for his friends" (John 15:13).

But right then in the Upper Room, Simon Peter, bless his heart, wanted to backtrack. Earlier, Jesus had said that a betrayer was in the room, and the rugged fisherman from Galilee wanted to make sure everyone knew that it wasn't him. He brags, undoubtedly with volume, that he won't ever deny Jesus. Like the rest, he hasn't made the connection between Judas' departure and Jesus' talk of a betrayer.

Peter's actions must have frustrated Jesus. He had just washed Peter's feet. The next day, he would die for the man. He has just given him an important, very simple command, but Peter didn't hear a word that he'd said. You can almost hear the anger in Jesus' voice as he tells Peter of a rooster yet to come, thereby silencing his protests (John 13:38).

"This is important, Peter! Why can't you get it? You're going to have to learn to love these men."

Wait a minute. Was Jesus talking to Peter . . . or to me?

Why is it so hard to hear, to understand, or to put it into practice? Here's the first condition of the promise: If we'll just love one another, we'll be blessed. Nevertheless, every generation, including ours, tends to shake off this command the way a duck shakes water off her back.

Like Peter, we go through a lot of unnecessary pain because we don't listen the first time.

Even John was slow to get it. The word *love* appears only six times in the first twelve chapters of John's gospel, twelve chapters that cover nearly three years of his walking with Jesus. Now, beginning with this Passover meal, John can finally hear Jesus speaking seriously of love just as surely as he can feel crisp air on his clean feet. John will write the word *love* an amazing thirty-one times in the next five chapters, a segment of Scripture that probably covered about six hours. From that night on, John never got over what Jesus called *agape* love. Years later, when he wrote the brief letters that make up part of our New Testament, he wrote the word *agape* some forty times!

It took a foot washing to drive home the point to John.

Can you love the betrayer in your life? Maybe a spouse walked out on you, or a business partner took your money. Your church kicked you out of the parsonage, your best friend slandered you. A boyfriend left you pregnant and penniless. Blatant discrimination floored you. Maybe the church leader you trusted let you down, or maybe it's something else. Perhaps the betrayal is driving a nail through your heart right now.

Life is full of disappointments and those who disappoint. Can you wash the feet of one who has hurt you? Jesus washed the feet of Judas Iscariot!

What about the slow learners in your life? You're a neat-freak, and he's a slob. The marriage is on hold while an all-out war wages over dirty clothes in the floor. Or maybe other teenagers are in the fast lane, and your mother can't bear to let you go. An older brother pretends that you're not alive. A sister-in-law ruins every holiday get-together.

They're tough cases, but can you patiently love these people, anyway? Jesus loved Simon Peter.

If you can love them all, betrayers and slow learners alike, you'll be blessed. Jesus makes that a promise. And here's the flip side of the promise: If you can't love the difficult people in your life, you'll miss the blessing. Jesus didn't make love an option. He called his instruction to us a *command*. The way a drill sergeant barks an order to a private, Jesus barks it to us. No excuses, no whining, no procrastination. Get it done, soldier! Love those folks around you.

Few joys in life are quite so precious as watching a friendship blossom, especially if it grows out of a manure pile. There's nothing like looking an adversary in the eye and loving him or her despite your differences of opinion. God's people can have a witness when they simply make it a habit to do exactly what Jesus asked us to do.

Stop reading this book. Make the commitment to love others. Love them, now.

Five

Laughing in the Face of Death

My friend Charlie Barfield had been through a tough week. First he underwent a double knee replacement. One knee at a time would have been more than enough trouble. I'm not saying that Charlie is a little old for that kind of surgery, but Charlie's dancing days were long past.

Then a week after the surgery, he had a heart attack during his rehabilitation work.

I went to see him in the hospital on Sunday afternoon, trying to cheer him up. It was a tough scene. Machines and intensive care nurses surrounded him, and tubes ran in and out of his body. Huge bandages covered his still-healing knees.

Charlie's wife had warned me that he was interested in his vital signs, so when I went in, I took a quick survey of the machines by his bed. Charlie's eyes were open, but a ventilator tube kept him from talking. Through eye movements, he let me know that he was alert.

"Hi, Brother Charlie," I said. "You're looking great."

Everything is relative, of course. If you had seen him a few days before, you'd understand my definition of *great.*

"Your blood pressure is great, your heart rate is fine—why Brother Charlie, people would pay lots of money for those kinds of vital signs. You're really doing great!"

Charlie started using sign language. He pointed to his bandaged knees, and he pointed to me. He pointed to his midsection and twirled his hand around in circles.

"You want a nurse, Brother Charlie?"

"No," he said with his eyes.

"Do you need something? Can I do something for you? Are you in pain?"

"No, you dummy, I'm trying to tell you something." Again, it was his eyes talking.

"Brother Charlie, I'm just not sure what you're saying."

He took my hand and started to spell. I worried about all the activity. He might have had good vitals, but he was recovering from a heart attack, and had all of these tubes, and the swelling around both knees. I hoped I wasn't getting him overexerted. He was spelling with his finger, and I was struggling to decipher what he wrote.

"S?"

His eyes said yes.

"W?"

Another winner.

"A?"

You're doing fine.

"P?"

That's right.

S-W-A-P. "Swap? You want me to swap with you?"

Charlie's eyes lit up over the joke, and somehow I knew that this man would be fine. Live or die, win or lose, when a man can laugh in the midst of adversity, his attitude will carry him where health care can't.

Christians should be able to laugh in the midst of adversity. Maybe it's not funny in the midst of the heart attack, and it's certainly not funny in the aftermath of tragic events. But if you think about it, no matter what happens, Christians will get the last laugh. Even when we die, we go to heaven!

My friend Bill Weeks was the pastor of a dynamic church, and I loved to visit him. He always had a mixture of good advice and bad jokes, punctuated with his distinctive laughter. No matter how bad the joke, you simply had to laugh with him.

Bill was diagnosed with cancer. One month later, he died. Between the time he received the news of his cancer and the funeral, I sat with him in his office. He was already very weak and was in the office only for a few minutes. We talked about the disease for a few minutes, and there was nothing funny about it.

Suddenly, Bill spun around in his pastor's chair, his eyes lit up, and he said, "You know, it's like a coin flip. Heads, I win . . . tails I win. Either way, I'm going to heaven!"

The passion of his statement winded him, but the thought of heaven thrilled him. As he read the passages on heaven in the Bible, he read of home. The glimpses of heaven energized him. In fact, Bill's death was no sad departure. At his own instruction, a jazz band played "When the Saints Go Marching In" to begin his funeral service. It wasn't hard to imagine Bill half dancing, half running across the golden streets of heaven, laughing at the thrill of simply being there.

I also remember the way my wife's grandmother died. The last few decades of her life had been filled with one illness and surgery and loss after another. For years, she had seen much pain and very little laughter.

She was expected to live another week, so the family members who gathered around her bed weren't expecting her imminent death. But as they talked, something caught their eyes. She smiled. She lit up like a kid coming down the stairs for Christmas morning . . . and then she was gone. Or, I should say, then she was *home.*

No wonder she smiled!

"In my Father's house are many rooms," Jesus said in John 14. "If it were not so, I would have told you. I am going there to prepare a place for you. And if I go and prepare a place for you, I will come back and take you to be with me that you also may be where I am."

Have you seen the architect's drawing of your new home? It's in Revelation 21. New Jerusalem, part of the new earth and the new heaven, is exemplary of the kind of care God will provide for us in eternity.

The city is a cube, as high as it is long and wide. Scholars have tried to put a physical dimension to it, but they all scratch their heads and wonder if it's possible. A city this size . . . well, only God could do this.

It measures fifteen hundred miles on all sides. If one corner of the city were placed on the southeastern corner of the United States, its southern wall would stretch from Jacksonville, Florida, to El Paso, Texas. From there, the city would go north through the heart of New Mexico, Colorado, Wyoming, and Montana and stretch three hundred miles into Canada. From there, the wall of New Jerusalem would stretch eastward through Canada until it turned south near Montreal. Its eastern wall would then follow the Appalachian Mountains through New York state, Virginia, both Carolinas, and Georgia as the square foundation was completed.

We can't imagine a city so large. But wait. We haven't considered its height! You wouldn't be able to see the top of it. You'd need the Space Shuttle to fly over it. Try to imagine looking fifteen hundred miles straight up!

I'm from the South, and I've been in several antebellum mansions. In such homes, the ceilings are high—very high. So let's do some math. If this new city, with all of these mansion-sized rooms, had twenty-foot-tall ceilings, elevators could stop at a whopping 396,000 floors! Laid out like a cube, the city would contain *billions* of square miles within its borders. Your new home would probably be bigger than your neighborhood, perhaps bigger than your entire town! No wonder the King James version calls these rooms "mansions." This is incredible!

As large as New Jerusalem is, that's just the city. Outside is the new earth. No ocean, just a perfect earth, paradise restored, watered by the River of Life that runs through it. Think of how wonderful it will be.

No pollution, war, or problems.

No doctors, chiropractors, pharmacies, dentists, bill collectors, or 1040 tax forms.

No telephone solicitations during dinner and no neighbor collecting for a favorite charity. In fact, there will be no collections for any charity of any kind, anywhere. There will be no police officers, firefighters, ambulance drivers, or insurance companies. There will be no lawyers, no politicians, and no television news reporters.

There will be church, but no offering will be taken. If you're not smiling by now, we're going to have to work really hard on you.

Christians simply have a good, long-range perspective on life. Life can throw some real problems at you, but the worst that life can do to you is kill you. Think about it: when we die, receiving the worst that life can give us—we go to heaven!

According to Acts 7, when Stephen saw heaven opening up, he no longer noticed the stones that were breaking his skull. It made a difference to Stephen when he got a glimpse of heaven.

Has it made a difference to you?

My friend Charlie got better, came home, and started walking on those two new knees. We talked about his humor in the hospital bed, and together we concluded that only Christians can laugh in the face of death. Only Christians. People who follow no particular faith or who follow any other religious belief can only *hope* that they'll be okay when they land on the "other side."

Christians *know.*

Jesus has gone before us, he's promised to come back for us, and he's been building the most incredible place for us that we could ever imagine. What if you had been in the Upper Room when Jesus first made this promise, when to all those anxious hearts he said,

> Do not let your hearts be troubled. Trust in God; trust also in me. In my Father's house are many rooms; if it were not so, I would have told you. I am going there to prepare a place for you. And if I go and prepare a place for you, I will come back and take you to be with me that you also may be where I am. You know the way to the place where I am going.
>
> —John 14:1–4

Would you have thrilled at the words? Would you have asked for a special feature in your new home? Or would you have wondered how it could all be possible?

Thomas is like most of us. He wanted clarification. He wanted signposts. He wanted clear directions. "Lord," Thomas said in John 14:5, trying to be polite, "we don't know where you are going, so how can we know the way?"

Jesus wasted no time with the reply: "I am the way and the truth and the life. No one comes to the Father except through me. If you really knew me, you would know my Father as well. From now on, you do know him and have seen him" (John 14:6–7).

As a people, we look for the right way in churches, in good works, in self-help books, and in our own intelligence. We listen for truth from politicians, philosophers, and preachers. We search for life in fitness centers, doctors' offices, and two-week vacations.

Jesus cuts right through all that we do, and he says, "It's me. I'm the One you're looking for. I'm the hope. I'm the peace. I'm the joy. I am the way, the truth, and the life. You're not going to find any way to eternal life or abundant life without me. It's me, me only, and me exclusively. If you want to get to the Father, if you want to get to all of those blessings you're after, you'll have to come through me. And if you want to go to heaven, you must come through me, and me alone."

You'll hear a lot of arguments, if you've not heard them yet, for the validity of other religions. Many other world religions take issue with Christians proclaiming that Jesus is the exclusive way of entering heaven. Because evangelical Christians continue to share their belief that Jesus is the *only* path to heaven, many world leaders act as though Christianity is a dangerous thing. What bothers me more, however, is that many *Christians* privately believe that God will, in the end, just smile on the lot of us and take us all into heaven.

Frankly, it takes less faith to believe what Jesus said in the Upper Room than it does to believe that God will write off the entire New Testament. It takes a lot of faith to believe that God will negate his own plan of salvation—the one that was in place the moment Adam and Eve took a bite of trouble in the Garden. God would have to ignore the perfect life of Jesus, the miraculous timing of all things miraculous, and even the cross.

Try to imagine a mother's grief when she hears that her only son died on a distant battlefield. Or picture that soldier's father as he reads the official letter announcing that a lifelong grief has begun. Now, try to imagine that they decide to forget the whole thing. "Let's just pretend he never lived," says the dad. "And let's certainly forget that he died in battle," agrees the mother.

What nonsense!

Will God the Father ever forget the cross?

We can pretend, hope, and pray all we want to for some other option. The truth is, the only way anyone will reach heaven is through faith in Jesus Christ.

Maybe you're still a bit like Thomas or Philip. Maybe you're like I was with eighth-grade algebra. All of the other students seemed to understand why $a + b = c$, but I was still looking for the numbers I'd known from our seventh-grade math classes. Once they mixed letters with numbers, I began to struggle.

There in the Upper Room, Thomas and Philip were stumped with the equation Jesus gave them. Thomas had asked the first question, so Philip was the next to raise his hand.

> Philip said, "Lord, show us the Father and that will be enough for us."
>
> Jesus answered: "Don't you know me, Philip, even after I have been among you such a long time? Anyone who has seen me has seen the Father. How can you say, 'Show us the Father'? Don't you believe that I am in the Father, and that the Father is in me? The words I say to you are not just my own. Rather, it is the Father, living in me, who is doing his work. Believe me when I say that I am in the Father and the Father is in me; or at least believe on the evidence of the miracles themselves. I tell you the truth, anyone who has faith in me will do what I have been doing. He will do even greater things than these, because I am going to the Father. And I will do whatever you ask in my name, so that the Son may bring glory to the Father. You may ask me for anything in my name, and I will do it."
>
> —John 14:8–14

Look at the words again and draw strength from them. Jesus began this passage by saying, "Do not let your hearts be troubled." It's as if he saw how anxious we are about dying, and he says, "Don't be anxious about this. This is not a reason for you to be uptight." The solution to our anxiety over death? "Trust in God; trust also in me."

Trust in God. Trust in the One who is so big that he could speak the universe into being. He is so big that he commands all of heaven, all of hell, and all of earth. He is totally in charge. He is the God of the Old Testament, the God of great miracles. By his instruction, through the power of his name, people walked to freedom through the sea. These same people won battles they should have lost. God's people survived multiple attempts to annihilate them. Now, says Jesus, trust in a God big enough to take care of you.

The problem in our relationship with God, however, is that we're constantly reminded of our failures. To be honest, the Old Testament conjures up more examples of great defeats than of great victories. While Moses took the Ten Commandments from God, God's people danced around a calf made of metal. Although David soared to great heights as a God-anointed king, he dropped like a stone when his eyes fixed on someone else's wife. After Israel's civil war, for every king who tried to walk with God, three ungodly kings led the people. In the end, the picture of failure is complete and convincing. We come away wondering if we'll ever match up to the requirements of this great God.

That's why in the Upper Room Jesus issued the second command: "Trust in me."

Jesus was human. He talked in stories, and he acted with authority. Miracles had marked his ministry and proved his divinity. But those around him had known him best through his deep friendship. Jesus loved them! They knew that one characteristic of Jesus better than any other. "If it scares you to think of dying and facing such a holy God," Jesus seems to be saying, "then trust in me. I love you. I am a reflection of the Father's love for you. He loves you so much, he sent me to you. He's got a job for me when I return to him. I'll be in the building business for a while, building a place for you. Do you know why? The Father and I want you to be there, with Us."

So don't let your heart be troubled. If you believe in Jesus as God's Son, if you've given control of your life to him, you can find joy even in the shadow of death.

Remember, this is a *conditional* promise. All of the promises of blessings, joy, and peace are dependent upon our willingness to do what Jesus commands. When Jesus says that he's the only way to get to heaven, believe him. When Jesus says, "Trust in God, trust in me," do it. Relax the way a child relaxes in the care of a loved one. If you can't believe, if you can't trust, don't expect to know peace in the face of death. Don't expect to have joy on your journey home. Don't plan on leaving this world for your eternal destination wearing a smile.

You *can* trust Jesus. You can know the blessing of assurance, no matter what happens in your life. Just ask my friend Charlie. Jesus makes all the difference in the world.

Consider this last story.

John Todd was a famous nineteenth-century clergyman. When he was just six, both of his parents died. A kindhearted aunt raised him until he left home to study for the ministry. Years later, the aunt became seriously ill, and in distress she wrote Todd a letter. The fear of death had stolen her laughter. Although she was a Christian, she had the questions that Thomas and Philip had. She had the same questions that you might have.

Would death, she asked, mean the end of everything, or could she hope for something beyond?

Todd quickly replied in a letter to his aunt:

It is not thirty-five years since I, as a boy of six, was left quite alone in the world. You sent me word you would give me a home and be a kind mother to me. I have never forgotten the day I made the long journey to your house. I can still recall my disappointment when, instead of coming for me yourself, you sent your servant, Caesar, to fetch me.

I remember my tears and anxiety as, perched high on your horse and clinging tight to Caesar, I rode off to my new home. Night fell before we finished the journey, and I became lonely and afraid. "Do you think she'll go to bed before we get there?" I asked Caesar. "Oh no!" he said reassuringly, "She'll stay up for you. When we get out o' these here woods, you'll see her candle shining in the window."

Presently, we did ride out into the clearing and there, sure enough, was your candle. I remember you were waiting at the door, that you put your arms close about me—a tired and bewildered little boy. You had a fire burning on the stove. After supper you took me to my new room, heard me say my prayers, and then sat beside me till I fell asleep.

Some day soon God will send for you, to take you to a new home. Don't fear the summons, the strange journey, or the messenger of death. God can be trusted to do as much for you as you were kind enough to do for me so many years ago. At the end of the road you will find love and a welcome awaiting, and you will be safe in God's care.[1]

Do you know what I thought the first time I read that story? One day, it's going to be good to get home!

Six

Laughing in the Deep End of the Pool

If ever I've been patient with each of my three daughters, it has been in a swimming pool. Learning how to swim, learning the fine art of diving, and mastering the deep end of a pool are some of the toughest lessons of trust in all of life.

As a boy, I was petrified in the swimming pool. Like most of the boys in my neighborhood, I was drawn to the city pool like a moth to flame. It was hot in South Georgia, and the pool was just around the block. The only problem was me. I didn't know how to swim. It took an entire summer for me to advance from floating in the shallow end to finally swimming with confidence in the deep end.

Before success, however, I experienced many failures. Once, I made a long line of swimmers climb back down the steps to the water slide. I had climbed to the top, but fear of what awaited me was greater than the embarrassment of climbing down in front of my peers. I was also the only kid in my Red Cross swimming class to fail diving. I just couldn't do it. At the time, the pain of belly flopping seemed less severe than the unknown of a headfirst dive. It took weeks before I mastered it.

But a funny thing happened on the way to the deep end of the pool. I trusted my teachers and discovered how much fun swimming can be. Ever since I sliced through the water with a painless, headfirst dive, and ever since I experienced the exhilaration of a slide into the pool, I've never gone back to failure. Belly flops are really painful! I'll do no more of those, thank you. And who'd want to back down from a water slide? Give me bigger, faster slides!

Those memories of my early attempts at swimming made me patient when each of my daughters forgot how to float as soon as I let go of her back. For all three, I treaded water and waited at the bottom of the slide, or near the diving board when each took the first big plunge. I shouted encouragement when they belly flopped ninety-nine times in a row.

Who knows? I thought. Number one hundred might be the magic dive!

When it came to his disciples, Jesus picked a bunch of belly floppers.

Thomas and Philip heard the truth as plainly as children hear swimming instructions. They had both seen miracles and evidence of the supernatural. They had both heard Jesus speak plainly about how to have eternal life and abundant life. They had been held afloat for three years, but now that Jesus was ready to let them go, they acted as if they'd never been in the water.

Jesus even refers to past lessons: "You know the way to the place where I am going" (John 14:4).

Imagine the scene. Thomas looks at Simon Peter, who's probably still wondering who the betrayer is. Philip has a puzzled look on his face, and behind him is a collage of blank faces.

Thomas said to [Jesus], "Lord, we don't know where you are going, so how can we know the way?"

Jesus answered, "I am the way and the truth and the life. No one comes to the Father except through me. If you really knew me, you would know my Father as well. From now on, you do know him and have seen him."

—John 14:5–6

Philip is having trouble with the deep end, too. He frames it politely, but Jesus keeps the intensity level high.

Philip said, "Lord, show us the Father and that will be enough for us."

Jesus answered: "Don't you know me, Philip, even after I have been among you such a long time? Anyone who has seen me has seen the Father. How can you say, 'Show us the Father'? Don't you believe that I am in the Father, and that the Father is in me? The words I say to you are not just my own. Rather, it is the Father, living in me, who is doing his work. Believe me when I say that I am in the Father and the Father is in me; or at least believe on the evidence of the miracles themselves. I tell you the truth, anyone who has faith in me will do what I have been doing. He will do even greater things than these, because I am going to the Father. And I will do whatever you ask in my name, so that the Son may bring glory to the Father. You may ask me for anything in my name, and I will do it."

—John 14:8–14

Time is running out for Jesus. We can hear the frustration in his voice. The men he has handpicked haven't made enough progress. In a few hours, they'll be swimming for their lives.

Think of all that Thomas and Philip had seen. Think of all that

James, John, and Peter had seen. None of the other disciples scolds the two who spoke. They're all having trouble at the moment, even though they've all seen convincing evidence that Jesus is the Son of God. Some even heard an audible voice from heaven, when the Father confirmed that Jesus is his Son. The scriptural record of that event shows that the disciples were profoundly shaken by the experience (see Luke 9:34–36).

They have seen Jesus

- heal several people with leprosy, the most gruesome disease of the day (Matt. 8:2–4; Luke 17:11–19);
- heal a centurion's servant simply by announcing the healing (Matt. 8:5–13);
- heal countless individuals, using only a spoken word or a simple touch, including one who was healed when she secretly touched Jesus (Matt. 9:20–22);
- heal at least seven blind men, the first time in history such healing had ever taken place (Matt. 9:27–31; 12:22; 20:29–34; Mark 8:22–26; John 9:1–7);
- heal several people who were crippled, including at least one man who was paralyzed (Matt. 9:2–7);
- calm a storm at sea (Matt. 8:23–27);
- walk on the water (Matt. 14:25); and
- feed huge crowds with ridiculously small amounts of food (Matt. 14:15–21; 15:32–38).

Some of them had felt the weight of their nets, full of fish, when Jesus caught a miracle for them.

They were all present when Jesus spoke a quiet word to a dead girl (Matt. 9:18–19, 23–25). With her grieving parents nearby, he brought her back to life! They were all there when Jesus stopped a funeral procession and gave a dead son back to his grieving mother (Luke 7:11–15). And a few weeks before that final Passover with Jesus, they had stood amazed in front of an open tomb. Four days had Lazarus been buried. After Jesus shouted his name, however, there was Lazarus, stumbling over the grave clothes and rubbing his eyes in the sunlight.

All of those events, and hundreds more that are not recorded for us, are wrapped up in a single sentence. Jesus said, "Believe me when I say that I am in the Father and the Father is in me; or at least believe on the evidence of the miracles themselves" (John 14:11).

Doubt is a terrible thing. Although it must pain God to see our doubting, doubt never hurts God. It always hurts us.

Remember when Jesus returned to Nazareth? He worshiped in his hometown, spoke to the crowd when he was asked to do so, and then listened to the cries of criticism. The people there simply would not believe that the Jesus who grew up in their community might actually be the Messiah.

Both Matthew and Mark record the results. Because of the unbelief of the people there, Jesus couldn't perform his usual array of miracles (see Matt. 13:54–58; Mark 6:1–5). Imagine the reality. People in Nazareth had arthritis, hearing deficiencies, sight loss, and intestinal disorders. If they had shown the slightest amount of faith, they could have been healed. Their neighbors in Magdala and Capernaum had already been, or soon would be, healed of such things. Folks in Nazareth, on the other hand, still hurt, limped, and squinted just as badly the day after Jesus left them as they had the day before he arrived. Their doubt didn't hurt Jesus; their doubt hurt them.

Doubt hounded the disciples all of the way to the cross, to the empty tomb, and even beyond it. At the very end of his story, Matthew tells us that some of them were still doubting *after the Resurrection* (Matt. 28:17)!

If eyewitnesses had trouble believing what they saw, it's little wonder that many Christians today struggle. But how frustrating it must be to the Lord when Christians today see the evidence of God at work all around them and wonder if what they see is real. How frustrating it must be for the Holy Spirit to hear a Christian assume that the abundant life is available for everyone but himself or herself. How frustrating it must be for Christ to see us standing on the foundation of two thousand years of church history and wondering if Christianity is relevant to the world today. How frustrating it must be for God to hear a Sunday regular pray, "Maybe next week I'll make the decision. . . ."

Here's the good news. Despite almost every one of us having times of doubt, God is patient. Like a swimming instructor calling out encouragement, Jesus tells us what could happen—if we'd just move beyond our doubt.

Do you remember what Jesus said?

> I tell you the truth, anyone who has faith in me will do what I have been doing. He will do even greater things than these, because I am going to the Father. And I will do whatever you ask in my name, so that the Son may bring glory to the Father. You may ask me for anything in my name, and I will do it.
>
> —John 14:12–14

Some of the disciples got it. Peter and John became famous for the miracles they performed in the name of Jesus, as did some of the other apostles. In time, the apostle Paul would perform amazing miracles. Once, for example, when Paul preached an exceptionally long sermon that lasted late into the evening, a young man fell sleep and tumbled out of a window to his death. Paul restored life to that young man (Acts 20:9–12). Perhaps another miracle is written between the lines of that Scripture. From that point, Pastor Paul preached shorter sermons!

James, the half-brother of the Lord, came to understand this particular blessing of asking in Jesus' name. Years later, when he wrote the book that bears his name, he said, "The prayer of a righteous man is powerful and effective" (James 5:16b). James had no doubt learned that from years of experience.

And it's true—if we believe in the promises of Jesus, and if we trust his instruction to us through the Holy Spirit, we'll be blessed in amazing ways.

What's the key to believing and trusting? Obeying the commands of Jesus. That's all we have to do. Jesus gave us the example by obeying the Father. "I do," he said, "exactly what my Father has commanded me" (John 14:31b). Months before, Jesus had said it this way:

> I tell you the truth, the Son can do nothing by himself; he can do only what he sees his Father doing, because whatever the Father does the Son also does.
>
> —John 5:19

And not long after that occasion, he said,

> When you have lifted up the Son of Man, then you will know that I am the one I claim to be and that I do nothing on my own but speak just what the Father has taught me.
>
> —John 8:28

So immersed was Jesus in doing exactly what the Father was doing that he constantly spoke of the Father. In fact, in John's gospel, Jesus spoke of the Father more than ninety times!

Here's the key to obeying the commands of Jesus: Let your mind dwell on the things of Christ with the same kind of constant passion that Jesus forced his mind to dwell on the Father. Take on, as Scripture says, "the mind of Christ." Know what will happen then? You'll love Jesus more and more, and you'll find yourself naturally doing what Jesus would do. As that happens, you'll begin reaping the blessings, the joy, and the peace that Jesus promised. You'll be swimming in the deep end of the pool.

Jesus said it should, and would happen . . . in your life.

> If you love me, you will obey what I command. And I will ask the Father, and he will give you another Counselor to be with you forever—the Spirit of truth. The world cannot accept him, because it neither sees him nor knows him. But you know him, for he lives with you and will be in you. I will not leave you as orphans; I will come to you. Before long, the world will not see me anymore, but you will see me. Because I live, you also will live. On that day you will realize that I am in my Father, and you are in me, and I am in you. Whoever has my commands and obeys them, he is the one who loves me. He who loves me will be loved by my Father, and I too will love him and show myself to him.
>
> —John 14:15–21

Many ways are open for you to take the leap of faith, sending you on the way to what Jesus called "abundant life."

The way a beginning swimmer works on coordinating arm strokes, breathing, and kicking, you could work on coordinating Bible study and prayer. The way a beginner keeps going back to the pool, you could continue attending a church that helps you understand. The way a new swimmer finally closes his eyes and dives headfirst into the deep end, you could take a deep breath and make a public declaration of your faith in Christ.

Perhaps you're further along than that in your spiritual swim. Maybe you're feeling as uncomfortable as those eleven disciples were in the Upper Room, hearing a challenge from Jesus to walk more deeply in faith, *right now.*

That was the real problem in the Upper Room. For the better part of three years, these men had been comfortable riding on the coattails of Jesus. He had done the miracles, and they had watched. He had healed the sick, and they had assisted happy family members. They brought the sack lunches, but Jesus had prayed them into feasts for thousands. Jesus had done the preaching, the teaching, and all of the confrontation. These disciples didn't like the idea that within hours, Jesus would no longer be with them. They didn't want to think of swimming alone in the deep end.

Something amazing happened, though. Fast-forward in the Bible, and in just a little more than seven weeks, Peter is boldly proclaiming the gospel, and the other ten disciples are baptizing three thousand new converts on a single afternoon. Miracle after miracle was performed by these once-doubting disciples. People were healed not only by their words or touch but, according to Acts 5:15, even by Peter's *shadow!* God did incredible things through the disciples. The church grew faster than the record-keepers could keep the numbers straight, and the new converts did wonderfully selfless acts. They sold land and property, giving the money to others who had need. They shared their food, their resources, and their friendship.

What made the difference? The Holy Spirit had arrived in a new and personal way. Jesus had promised that the Counselor would come and that this Helper would make all of the difference. Jesus was gone, and the Holy Spirit was present. The book of Acts is so filled with the resulting miracles that some people have suggested that it be called "The Book of Miracles."

To complete the illustration, these eleven disciples became excellent swimmers. They mastered the pool, moved to the lake, and then tackled the ocean. They were the Iron Men of the faith, those who could endure and compete and win great championships. Despite their continuing faults and weaknesses, they overcame all of their doubts and became known as great people of faith.

That could be you.

If you haven't learned how to swim, learn. If you're still frightened to take that first dive, jump. If you've mastered the pool, tackle the lake. If the lake is easy for you, move to the ocean. Do not fear, because Jesus is watching over you, even as a lifeguard would watch over the beach. His last words spoken on earth, according to Matthew's record, should give you comfort: "And surely I am with you always, to the very end of the age" (Matt. 28:20b).

Why are you waiting? Go on. Get into the water!

Seven

An Offer of Peace

I'll bet you've never felt sorry for dirt.

Every spring, the ritual of farming begins. Farmers crank up their tractors, gardeners start their tillers, and homeowners take a hoe to the pansy patch at the front door. The plow slices into ground, the tiller starts to churn, and the hoe begins to chop.

The dirt is thrown into a turmoil. It is moved to a new location. Chunks of earth become broken into tiny pieces. One moment, the soil was basking in the sun, the next moment it is violently displaced. It has no control over its displacement and is at the complete mercy and will of the one doing the churning.

Centuries ago, Greek farmers had a word for what happened to the dirt under the plow. They called it *tarasso*. The ground, they said, was "troubled." *Tarasso*. The fields weren't just slightly bothered by the plow—they were broken and tossed and turned and forced to obey the will of the plow.

Fishermen used the same word to describe the water when a

sudden storm blew in. As the water went from glassy stillness to heaving waves, it was "troubled." *Tarasso.*

Dirt and water aren't the only things that can be plowed up or tossed around. Hearts can suffer the effects of *tarasso,* too. Sometimes the troubling of a heart can come quickly and unexpectedly, the way it happened on September 11, 2001, when we watched terrorists fly airplanes into American landmarks. Sometimes, the troubling comes from years of watching crime rates soar and reading decades of horrible headlines in the daily newspaper.

Sometimes the evidence is in our own neighborhoods.

Ride around . . . or simply go home. You'll see security guards posted at the entrances of some residential communities. In other places you might see electronic, steel gates sliding into place in front of apartment complexes. The cars that roll past those gates also have security systems ready to sound the alarm at the first sign of trouble.

From the most modest of homes to the wealthiest of America's neighborhoods, home security systems are on guard throughout every block. Motion detectors watch entranceways and family rooms. Doorways are armed to scream at the first unauthorized entrance. Windows are sealed by wireless sensors. Outdoor motion sensors alert homeowners of footsteps on the walk before the doorbell ever rings. Large, trained guard dogs become more than family pets. They are family protectors.

From steel bars across windows to deadbolts on the doors to high-tech, video-surveillance cameras, America attempts to sleep peacefully during unpeaceful, *tarasso* times.

For this "peace of mind," Americans shelled out more than $15 billion for home security systems in 1999 alone. The price tag for peace at home has risen 47 percent in just five years. The statistic is astounding for not only the sharp rise in what we're spending for home security but also because the price of security systems has plummeted over that same period.[1]

Before every ball game we sing about living in the land of the free. But most of us have made small fortresses out of our homes. If you thumb through a security company's pamphlets, it looks like we're bunkering in for war.

How ironic—considering our frenzied search for peace—that we are so much *not* at peace. Our hearts have been plowed through by the fear of violence, and our still waters are stirred and stormy because of stressful national and international tensions, or because of conditions at work, at school, or at home. In fact, it seems that family relationships can erode faster than a springtime rain erodes a hillside.

Sometimes, even a safe harbor like the church becomes a place where trouble develops.

Whatever the reason, we all understand *tarasso*. So did the eleven men who remained in the Upper Room with Jesus.

For some three years, these men had walked with Jesus throughout Israel, for the most part without fear of the stresses around them. The water of their lives had been still and pleasant. They weren't afraid of the Roman soldiers, the Jewish religious leaders, or the bandits in the hills. Every time a storm had blown in, Jesus had calmed it with a word. Every time the authorities got too close, Jesus had either sent them away embarrassed or won them over. These men had grown accustomed to living as untroubled as the dirt in an untilled meadow.

In the span of a few days, however, a plow had arrived. A storm of public criticism had blown in faster than they could comprehend. Jesus said that one from their midst was a betrayer, that others around the table would deny him. The disciples were feeling depressed, gathered inside a private, darkened room, in part to eat a Passover meal but hiding, too, from the executioners who lurked somewhere in Jerusalem.

They had never experienced such stress, and it was about to get worse. The storm of public opinion was about to turn into a hurricane of nightmarish proportions. Jesus would be beaten nearly to death and then hung on a cross, suffering his last six hours in agony. His mother would scream her grief at the foot of the cross, and his men would scatter like cockroaches under a bright light.

They would vomit their self-hatred in dark alleys and battle hysteria during a sleepless weekend. None of the disciples would even take the risk of burying their friend. They left that task to two newcomers—Joseph of Arimathea and Nicodemus—and to the women who dressed the body. The disciples were so filled with fear, so undone by trouble, so shaken by the *tarasso* that they let the man they had once called "Messiah" be buried without their presence.

If, by chance, life has put you in a troubling moment, listen to what Jesus promised. If, by chance, your heart is displaced or stormy, claim the gift that Jesus offered. If you think there's no peace for you, remember that in the Upper Room, the very chamber of fear, Jesus first offered it to these eleven men. Judas was gone, and only believers were left to hear the truth.

> All this I have spoken while still with you. But the Counselor, the Holy Spirit, whom the Father will send in my name, will teach you all things and will remind you of everything I have said to you. Peace I leave with you; my peace I give you. I do not give to you as the world gives. Do not let your hearts be troubled and do not be afraid.
>
> —John 14:25–27

Peace. This was the second of three promises that Jesus gave on this, the last night of his life. He promised blessings, peace, and joy. And that's what we want. Who wouldn't want to live in peace? You want it. I want it!

Jesus says, "Take it!" Let's expand on his words for a moment.

"Don't let your hearts be continually plowed up by anxiety or strife," is what the Lord was saying. "Don't let a storm of anger toss your emotions around in an uncontrolled way. Don't let fear so control your life that your heart is constantly timid. Don't be ruled by the fear that can steal your dreams. I can give you peace— peace that will make a difference in those circumstances of life."

Wouldn't you like that?

This peace is not as hard to have as most people think. Go back in the passage just a bit, and hear one of those rather timid, troubled hearts ask a question:

> Then Judas (not Judas Iscariot) said, "But, Lord, why do you intend to show yourself to us and not to the world?"
>
> Jesus replied, "If anyone loves me, he will obey my teaching. My Father will love him, and we will come to him and make our home with him. He who does not love me will not obey my teaching. These words you hear are not my own; they belong to the Father who sent me."
>
> —John 14:22–24

Don't miss this. The one and only condition of finding the peace that Jesus offered is simply to obey the commands of Jesus, which are the commands of God.

You've probably noticed that obedience is a key theme throughout these last hours of Jesus' teaching. The word *obey* appears eight times in these four chapters, all of them coming between that final Passover meal and Jesus' arrest a few hours later.

Obedience is, in fact, practically synonymous with following Jesus. In Revelation 12:17 and 14:12, for instance, one who keeps the commands of God is equal to one who belongs to God. And that is perhaps the best way to interpret the parable of the sheep and goats in Matthew 25. Sheep were recognized as sheep because of what they *had* done, and goats were cast away because of what they *hadn't* done. Obedience is the stamp of authenticity that shows that Jesus owns your heart.

Explaining the tension between good works and salvation is like walking a tightrope. It's difficult to explain that our good works have nothing to do with getting us to heaven, yet because of our good works we'll be known as God's children.

Maybe some illustrations will help. How do you recognize soldiers? By their uniforms, their way of marching, a way of doing certain tasks, and a willingness to follow orders from a commander, even if the orders put the soldiers in harm's way.

How do you recognize a married person? By a wedding ring, perhaps, or more certainly by his or her actions. He or she doesn't date anyone else after the marriage and is faithful to the spouse day in and day out. The words, the photo in the purse or wallet, and the smile when he or she calls the spouse's name tell the world that the person is married.

How can you tell if a young man is suddenly in love? For the first time in his life, he's a customer at the florist shop. He checks the theater listings in the newspaper for a movie *she'd* like to see. He changes his daily schedule, eats less, sleeps less, and smiles constantly.

So how does one join the armed forces? One signs up. How does one become married? By agreeing to the covenant and saying "I do" on the wedding day.

One must enter into the service of the army or into the bonds of marriage. After entry into the service or into marriage—and *only* after—actions occur that identify the one who willingly entered the terms of the agreement. No one becomes a soldier by marching down the street by himself. No one becomes married simply by buying a wedding ring and wearing it. No young man has ever begun shopping at the florist, thinking, "If I just buy enough flowers, maybe I'll fall in love."

No, actions are indeed defining, but only after what has happened in each life. One enlists and therefore acts like a soldier. One repeats vows at the wedding and is therefore married. He spotted her, flipped, and fell in love.

The only way a person can become a Christian is to enter willingly into a covenant with Jesus Christ. He died for us on the cross and, in a sense, proposed to us: "Would you be mine?" If we take Jesus' offer, we have entered into the agreement, *immediately being guaranteed an eternal home in heaven.* And after that entry point, our actions will define how seriously we took the offer from Christ.

No one becomes a Christian by performing actions. You can't go to church enough, can't give enough money, and can't do enough good things. It is only through "signing-up" or "taking the vow" that you become a child of God. But the actions that follow should be as noticeably changed as are the actions of a new recruit, a newlywed, or a young man who is in love.

Let's take the illustrations a bit further. The more conscientiously a soldier follows commands in the armed services, the more likely he or she is to make advancements in the service. He'll be promoted. She'll take on new responsibilities. In a marriage, the more each spouse works on the marriage, the better the marriage will be. The better the communication, the better the relationship. The kinder the words, the softer the touch, the better the romance. The more time a young man spends in dating the girl he's in love with, the more he'll be able to determine if the relationship will blossom into marriage. For all three examples, rewards result from working hard at this new lifestyle. Similarly, the more you follow the commands of Jesus, the more peace will be an obvious part of your life.

On the last night of his earthly life, in his most serious teaching ever, Jesus used the word *obey* eight times. Here's a sampling:

If you love me, you will obey what I command.

—John 14:15

Jesus replied, "If anyone loves me, he will obey my teaching."

—John 14:23

He who does not love me will not obey my teaching.

—John 14:24

As the Father has loved me, so have I loved you. Now remain in my love. If you obey my commands, you will remain in my love, just as I have obeyed my Father's commands and remain in his love.

—John 15:9–10

The lesson is unavoidable and unmistakable. Jesus offers us peace, and that peace relates directly to the effort we exert in obeying him. A Christian who never attends church, never reads his or her Bible, never spends time in the prayer closet, and who never or rarely makes an effort to grow in obedience shouldn't expect to have much peace in life. In fact, internal turmoil will be a way of life for that person.

Will we avoid trouble in life? Of course not. Can we escape grief? Not if we live long enough. Will our peaceful existence ever be plowed under? Sure it will, and probably at some point it already has been.

Is the promise of Jesus still true even during times of trouble? Bank on it. Count on it. Take it personally. Jesus can still give you peace. Obey his commands and bask in that peace. Jesus said that you could have it and could choose it—right now.

All this I have spoken while still with you. But the Counselor, the Holy Spirit, whom the Father will send in my name, will teach you all things and will remind you of everything I

have said to you. Peace I leave with you; my peace I give
you. I do not give to you as the world gives. Do not let your
hearts be troubled and do not be afraid.

—John 14:25–27

According to what Jesus says, two things will be done for you,
and one thing you'll have to do for yourself. If you choose to receive the two and do the other, you'll have this promised peace.

First, the Holy Spirit will be with you as a helper, a teacher, and
a reminder. You're not going to be alone. The presence of God
will literally be with you through the reality of the Holy Spirit. As
you accept the invitation to become a Christian, you receive the
certainty of both eternal life and the Holy Spirit. As you obey the
teachings of Christ, as you continue to take bigger and bigger
steps of faith, you will be more and more aware of the Holy Spirit.
Again, obedience is the major prerequisite.

Second, simply rest in the knowledge that Jesus has already
made this peace available: "Peace I leave with you; my peace I
give you."

What's your part? Receive the gift.

Think of it this way. A boy's father tells him, "There's a new car
for you parked in the carport." The boy can sit in the house for
years, if he wants, and wonder if his father's promise is really true.
Or he can choose to go out to the carport and claim the promise.
Can you imagine any boy wondering for very long if the promise
of a new car was true? Even if the "new" car was an old rattletrap
with a worn-out engine, he'll race outside and receive the gift with
joy. Imagine how our Father feels when Christians sit inside their
houses, fearful and wondering if this gift of peace is real.

I repeat—receiving this gift of peace is indeed up to you. "Do
not let your hearts be troubled and do not be afraid," Jesus said.
Put another way, you must make the choice not to be ruled by
anxiety, stress, or fear. Those things create a "timid" heart, Jesus

said, the only time that Greek word was used in all of the Gospels. You must make an intentional choice to rejoice, despite the circumstances of life.

If you're a believer, the Holy Spirit is alive in you right now. By obeying the commands of Christ you'll become even more aware of the Holy Spirit's presence. One of the commands of Christ is to choose *not* to be anxious. But we—you and I—must first make that choice. If we do, we'll find peace. And we can leave *tarasso* for the dirt!

Eight

Laughter Is a Battle

It was a cold, rainy January morning—the kind best spent with a cup of coffee and the morning paper. That's one of my favorite daily activities. The sports section that particular week was obsessed with Super Bowl XXXIV, in which the two best teams in the National Football League would battle it out in Atlanta, a relatively short drive from our home.

Since we didn't have tickets, I already knew we wouldn't be battling the traffic or the crowds on game day. Instead, we'd probably build a fire in the fireplace, enjoy some chili, and watch the game on TV with friends. But on that morning, days before the game began, I saw the promises of Jesus right there in the sports section.

The sports section? No, I haven't overdosed on Wheaties or consumed too much Gatorade. It makes perfect sense. In fact, finding Jesus in the sports section is a valuable lesson in itself. The principles of the Bible are rarely lived out in sterile, stained-glass environments. They're usually demonstrated by regular Joes and Janes, sometimes for the whole world to see. The example in the sports page was a vivid one.

The starting quarterbacks of the two Super Bowl teams were in the spotlight, soaking up the thrill of making it to the top of their profession and earning thousands of dollars in the process. The laughter came easily that week for Kurt Warner and Steve McNair. Fans who weren't familiar with the whole story might think that Warner and McNair were the typical big stars, with big egos, making big money by using their golden arms to throw footballs to other big-time egos. Those same fans might think that these two quarterbacks had just waltzed through life into the biggest dance of the season.

But it had been far from a dance. Aside from the years of practice, workouts, and hours of weight-lifting, both players had almost been ignored by college football's elite teams. Instead of playing before eighty thousand fans every Saturday with other future NFL stars, both of these quarterbacks had played before smallish crowds in Division I-AA—college football's second tier. McNair found a home at Mississippi's Alcorn State, and Warner played on the frozen fields of Northern Iowa. The only way these two college quarterbacks had been involved in bowl games was by flipping from one channel to another on New Year's day.

Warner's story is the one in which I'd taken a particular interest. Coming out of college, Warner tried to make the Green Bay Packers, but the Packers cut him. Warner's missing the team roster didn't surprise anyone. Until his fifth year, Warner didn't start even for Northern Iowa. After the Packers cut him, Warner got a minimum-wage job stocking groceries at a local supermarket in Cedar Falls, Iowa. His life revolved around cans of green beans, boxes of disposable diapers, and jars of peanut butter. He finally got a chance to play quarterback in the Arena Football League, and later he played with NFL Europe.

But when Warner was in camp with the St. Louis Rams in 1999, the team's starting quarterback suffered a season-ending injury during a preseason game. Suddenly, Warner had his chance.

As the season unfolded, Warner threw forty-one touchdown passes, only the second quarterback in NFL history to throw that many. He ran away with the season's Most Valuable Player award. Then he led the Rams through the playoffs to their first-ever Super Bowl appearance as a St. Louis team. Once there, Warner threw the late, game-winning touchdown in the Super Bowl, taking home the Super Bowl MVP trophy, too.

It was a far cry from beans and baby food.

But the reason Warner drew my attention, making me so aware of the promises of Jesus, is that Warner is an outspoken Christian. He didn't make much money in his rags-to-riches season (he was signed to the NFL's minimum salary contract), but he did make the most of every opportunity to share his faith with those who would listen.

"The biggest thing I've learned is the Lord has a plan for me," he said in newspaper interviews. "I've learned about being humble and enjoying everything you've got. I've learned a lot and I've grown through the experience."[1]

He's not kidding. During this Super Bowl run, Warner and his wife really wanted to enjoy Christmas. So you know what they did? They took their children to a nearby nursing home for Christmas Day. They loaded up their van with gifts for every single nursing home resident and spent the day there talking with folks who, for the most part, didn't have a clue who he was. There were no television cameras or *Sports Illustrated* reporters to record the incident, just visiting family members on Christmas Day, surprised by the generosity of a man they didn't even know. Warner also promised, midway through the season, to give any midseason raise to his family's favorite charity, a summer camp for handicapped children.

He's done more, but here's the point: Warner's actions weren't designed to produce peace in his life. The reverse is true. His peace, the result of the difference that Christ had made in his life years earlier, produced his actions, which were different than many people would have expected. He might have been laughing in the Super Bowl, but earning that laughter had been a real battle.

Warner's success was reported in the sports pages. But, from the pages of our own experiences and from the pages of the Bible, many of us learn that early adversity sweetens the taste of success. Warner undoubtedly felt satisfaction with racking up points in football, and we score points of satisfaction in our lives—and perhaps you already have—but those points don't come quickly or cheaply.

Consider Jesus. To give this peace, he had to endure the cross.

To receive the peace and joy that Jesus offered, the disciples had to endure a weekend of hellish proportions. They went through a period of hopelessness, two days and two nights of despair and fear.

And to receive the peace that passes all comprehension you, too, might have to endure a season of pain, hopelessness, or despair.

Hang on. As truly as resurrection Sunday arrived for the disciples, peace is coming for all believers who will endure through the tough times.

The weekend of the crucifixion must have been a nightmare for the disciples. Beginning early Friday, they lost their voices because of the horror of the cross. There were no joyous miracles on Friday, in the supernatural darkness, the earthquake, and the storm. The night before, Jesus had washed their feet. By Friday afternoon, he was stiff and lifeless, scarred almost beyond recognition.

Saturday was the longest day that any of them had ever lived. They couldn't travel without being recognized because Jews didn't travel on the Sabbath. If they had moved along the highways, they would have stood out like fugitives running from crosses. They hid, they wept, and they skipped meals. Did they know how to pray on that Sabbath?

Perhaps the only thing that kept them breathing was that Jesus had so often told them that this day was coming. Even on the night before his death, Jesus had repeated that prophecy. John heard it and wrote it on his heart. By Sunday morning, he was able to go into the tomb, comprehend the facts quickly, and become the first disciple to believe that Jesus had, indeed, been raised from the dead.

Again, rewind the Scripture to that Upper Room. Listen to Jesus as he looks his men in the eyes and tells them what is about to happen.

> You heard me say, "I am going away and I am coming back to you." If you loved me, you would be glad that I am going to the Father, for the Father is greater than I. I have told you now before it happens, so that when it does happen you will believe. I will not speak with you much longer, for the prince of this world is coming. He has no hold on me, but the world must learn that I love the Father and that I do exactly what my Father has commanded me.
>
> Come now; let us leave.
>
> —John 14:28–31

Jesus told them then, as he had before, that a tough time lay ahead. He also assured them that, in the long run, they would be glad about all of the coming events, even though some of those events would be horribly painful. They would actually come to rejoice about the weekend ahead of them, the way an ecstatic new father bounds out of his house to tell the world that his first child has been born.

Jesus must have been looking into some pretty confused faces, but he had to continue. The time for the battle was rapidly approaching.

Before they left the room, Jesus said one thing that should have shot chills through their hearts: "I will not speak with you much longer, for *the prince of this world is coming.*"

The disciples knew that Jesus was talking about Satan. The Pharisees, the religious leaders of the day, often referred to Satan as "the prince." On more than one occasion, these leaders had accused Jesus of being in cahoots with the Devil: "It is by the prince of demons that he drives out demons," they said in Matthew 9:34. Jesus had also referred to Satan as "the prince of this world" in John 12:31. So when Jesus said, "the prince of this world is coming," they knew they were all about to have an encounter with the Devil.

But before they could digest that bit of bad news, Jesus assured the disciples that he—not Satan—would remain in control. *"He has no hold on me,* but the world must learn that I love the Father and that I do exactly what my Father has commanded me."

From the beginning of Jesus' life, Satan had been on a mission to destroy him. Herod's butchering of babies in Bethlehem was an attempt to kill the child Jesus. By the time he reached Nazareth, the home of his childhood, Jesus had already been taken to Egypt and back. In fact, angels were on guard, warning Mary and Joseph of every move they must make and make quickly. When Jesus began his ministry, there was the Evil One, throwing out his best temptations, trying to stop God's plan of mercy in its tracks. For three years, Jesus had gone throughout Israel, healing the sick, preaching . . . and encountering demons. They recognized him, they shrieked at him, and they obeyed his commands to vacate their victims. In short, the Prince of Darkness had been after Jesus from the moment he was born, and every minute of his life thereafter.

Now Satan was throwing everything he had into nailing Jesus to a cross. It would not be enough to kill the Son of God. Satan wanted Jesus to be publicly displayed as a trophy kill. He wanted to celebrate as no enemy of God had ever celebrated.

On the other hand, Jesus wanted the disciples to know that the apparent loss was, in reality, a victory. Satan had not won the battle on the cross, and he never would. Imagine what happened when the last words Jesus uttered on earth echoed through every dark corner of hell: *"Tetelestai*—It . . . is . . . *finished."*

Satan swallowed his laughter. His heart skipped a beat. He gasped for air as he comprehended the words: *"It* is finished." In that one moment, Satan's biggest victory turned into his own death sentence. The defeat was final, and the celebration would begin on Sunday . . . *Super Sunday.*

But before it all transpired, Jesus wanted those disciples to know there in the Upper Room that even if it seemed that the prince of this world had won a battle, the opposite was true. Jesus faced his toughest battle knowing that his greatest victory lay just ahead.

Jesus wanted his followers to know something else. The same kind of attacks would come upon not only them but also upon all of those who would follow Christ. As Jesus chose to follow the commands of the Father, we today can choose to follow Jesus. At every stage of life, we can yield to the Evil One—or be blessed by the touch of the Messiah. In a sense, a constant battle is being waged for your laughter.

Only a few months before his crucifixion, Jesus plainly had laid out the purpose of that battle: "A thief is only there to steal and kill and destroy. I came so they can have real and eternal life, more and better life than they ever dreamed of" (John 10:10 *The Message*).

The abundant life is a life so full that it can hardly be described. Imagine a glass of water filled so full that the water level appears to be *above* the rim of the glass. One more drop and water will certainly spill down the side. Then Jesus comes along and says, "You want to see full? Watch this." Then he takes a full pitcher of water and pours it into that already-full glass. Water cascades everywhere, and the glass is still gloriously full. It cannot possibly hold all of the fullness.

"That," says Jesus, "is what I'm offering you."

The thief, Satan, wants to rob you of that experience. He wants to steal everything he can from you. He wants to destroy your joy, put a lid on your laughter. He'll come into the tough circumstances of your life and remind you of how bad things are. He'll provide all of the party favors and black balloons for your pity party. He'll do this even if you are a Christian! If the Devil loses the battle for your soul, he will do everything possible to take away your abundant life. Don't let it happen.

John, Peter, Andrew, Paul, and Silas—all of them—suffered great physical and emotional discomfort for the rest of their lives. They endured trials and prison terms. They were whipped, stoned, and beaten. They lost friends who were killed for the sake of the gospel. According to tradition, all of the disciples, except John, were executed. John's punishment was banishment to a lonely island, where he was sent to die. But through all of those attacks, the apostles possessed abundant life.

You probably read those last few sentences too quickly. We skim through the accounts of hardship in Scripture the way we scan bad news in the headlines. When the earthquake happens on the other side of the world, when an act of terrorism happens in another city, when the traffic accident claims the life of someone we don't know, or when the fire burns down a stranger's home, we take in the information and miss the pain. We're conditioned to do that. We couldn't possibly handle that much pain.

Sooner or later, however, pain comes home. Maybe it's a crisis, like an accident, a fire, or an earthquake. Maybe it's a gall-bladder attack that wrings you out and tosses you to the floor like a limp dishrag. Perhaps you're experiencing conflict at work, and you've been summoned to a meeting. Maybe it's the call from the doctor's office asking for a meeting later in the day, and something in the nurse's voice warns you that it's bad news. Perhaps your fiancée tells you that the relationship is over, or maybe your spouse announces that the marriage is over. Perhaps a morning argument leaves you full of tension until the problem can be resolved by day's end.

No matter what the situation, the truth remains as Jesus warned us—your enemy, the Devil, wants to steal your joy, kill your peace, and destroy your laughter. Watch out for him. Battle him. Make that choice to rejoice in the middle of the tough times, and claim the abundant life. You might not laugh out loud, and you certainly won't enjoy the pain that comes as part of life. Jesus, remember, didn't laugh on the last night of his life. He faced his pain honestly and openly, and he hurt as much as you or I would.

But here's something remarkable about the Bible. God's Word will never make light of your difficult circumstances. The Bible is honest about the pain that comes upon us all. Many of the psalms were sung by weeping singers. In fact, an entire book in the Bible is called Lamentations. Jesus once wept as he grieved, the way any man grieves, when his closest friend died.

The lesson in the midst of your pain? Do not lose your faith! By the end of the weekend, a resurrection could happen.

*   *   *

Our party was over. We'd eaten and laughed our way through the Big Game. The fire was dying, the food was gone, and the end of the Super Bowl had come with a rare, thrilling finish. Now there wasn't much left to see, but we all waited for the television reporter to find Kurt Warner. Politically correct TV reporters often try to avoid talk of religion, and this one was no exception. All week long Warner had made no bones of his faith, bringing talk of Jesus into every Georgia Dome interview. Kurt's wife had already given a revival-style testimony during the game when interviewed in the stands. Now, at the end of the game, you could tell the reporter wanted to talk about football and football only. After all, this was a *game,* not church. *Surely,* the TV interviewer must have thought, *the Bible can take a backseat to that great, fourth-quarter, game-winning, Hall-of-Fame, highlight-film, touchdown bomb.*

"Kurt, first things first," began the reporter with the microphone connected to the entire world. "You've got to tell us about that game-winning pass."

"First things first?" Warner said, almost laughing out loud at the easy opening. At that moment, the man who had endured such hardship, the man who had found such a genuine faith in the midst of pain, the man who had found such abundant life *away* from the games, reared his head back and shouted from the depth of his satisfied soul, "Thank you, JEEE-SUSSSS!"

And the sound of his joy reverberated around every stadium corridor and through the speakers of two hundred million television sets—and right into the heart of heaven.

Nine

"Come Now; Let Us Leave"

E very young man who's hidden an engagement ring in his pocket knows it. Every woman who's ever composed a resume understands it. Every baseball pitcher who's ever started the big game comprehends it.

In the pursuit of every dream, you've got to take the first step. You can talk, pray, hope, dream, and plan for only so long.

Sooner or later, you've got to pop the question. One day you've got to mail the resume. When the umpire yells, "Play ball," you have to rear back and let 'er rip. Whatever happens after that happens only *after* the first step.

Jesus was in the middle of his most serious teaching ever, and he still had a lot to say. He would squeeze in critically important information while he walked into the night with eleven followers. He would speak as slowly as possible, yet with an increasing passion, hoping that young John was going to retain it verbatim.

No one else said what only Jesus could say that night. No one else *could* have said it.

The cross was there for Jesus, not for John, James, Peter, Andrew, or the rest. The arrest, the challenge in the garden, the ordeals of interrogation—they were was all meant for Jesus. Therefore, only Jesus could say the words that end the fourteenth chapter of John: "Come now; let us leave."

To reach the reality of the promises he was making, Jesus had to put his feet on the floor, gather his cloak, and walk out the door. He had to walk toward his arrest, toward the beatings, toward the cross. He knew full well what lay ahead of him. As they left the city, Jesus and the disciples probably made a wide circle around the Temple Mount, skirting the trouble that might await them. If so, it's conceivable that they walked within eyesight of the Valley of Gehenna before descending into the Kidron Valley.

Picture the Valley of Gehenna. That's where people threw their garbage. That's where the sewage got dumped. That's where the bodies of rotting animals were tossed. It was a low, dark, deadly place. They called it *Gehenna* because that was their word for *hell*.

Considering where they were heading, it must have been a strange invitation to hear, "Come now; let us leave."

There *has* to be a lesson in this powerful little statement. I think it concerns attitude as much as it does actions. If surgery's in store, face it with a smile. Be an example to your friends and family members who are watching. If the lay-off list has your name on it, choose optimism instead of profanity.

Late in his life, while giving instructions for overcoming anxiety, Paul wrote, "Let your countenance be known to all men; the Lord is near" (Phil. 4:5 NEW AMERICAN STANDARD BIBLE).[1] Other translations say it this way:

> Let your gentleness be evident to all. . . .
>
> —NEW INTERNATIONAL VERSION

Let your forbearing spirit be plain to every one. . . .
                          —TWENTIETH CENTURY NEW TESTAMENT[2]

Let your moderation be known. . . .
                                        —KING JAMES VERSION

Let your humility be known. . . .
                                                  —LAMSA[3]

Have a reputation for gentleness. . . .
                          —NEW TESTAMENT IN MODERN ENGLISH[4]

In other words, when it's time to go toward what you know will
be difficult, do what Jesus did: pick up your cloak and, without
panic or fear, head toward your future.

How did Jesus walk so confidently toward the cross? He had
his mind set on his resurrection and the triumph of the Father's
plan of salvation. His attitude was perfect.

How will you walk in confidence toward your future? Focus on
the blessings, the peace, and the joy that Christ offers. Focus on
the fact that Jesus has walked first, inviting us to *come with him.*
We don't have to travel alone. It might be dark, descending into
the valley of hell, but at least we're not alone. Jesus promised that
he would never, ever leave us. As Paul said in that tiny verse of
Philippians, let your countenance be know to all men, a countenance of confidence that knows, in faith, that "the Lord *is* near."

Let his attitude be your cloak. Let his sandals guide your footsteps. And as you go, remember that the laughter is just beyond
the pain. Just beyond the cross is a resurrection. Just beyond the
grief is wild celebration. Focus on the laughter that is to come.

But it won't come without that important first step. So grab
your cloak, strap on your sandals—and *get it done.*

Ten

The Laughter of Bearing Fruit

Dr. Don Harper Mills, president of the American Association of Forensic Science, attests that the following story is true. It's the story of Ronald Opus, who lay dead on an examining table. Dr. Mills was trying to reach a conclusion about this man's death, which had occurred during what can only be termed as bizarre circumstances. The date of the examination was March 23, 1994.

The obvious conclusion was that Ronald Opus had died of a shotgun wound to the head. But the whole story is complicated. Opus had jumped from a ten-story building, intent on committing suicide. He left a note revealing his depression and his intention to end his life. Then he jumped.

On the way to a certain death on the street below, he passed a ninth-story window. As he fell past the window, a shotgun blast ended his life. In a twist of irony, a safety net had been stretched alongside the wall on the seventh floor, placed there for some workers. Opus didn't know about the net when he jumped. If he had not been shot, he would have been saved by the net! Now the coroner needed to answer the tricky and important question of whether Opus died of a homicide or a suicide.

The occupants of the room where the gun shot came from were an elderly man and his wife. They had been arguing when the old man began waving a shotgun at his wife. The gun went off, missing her completely, but hitting poor Opus as he plunged toward a seventh-floor safety net.

According to the law, the elderly man could now be charged with murder because he had fired a gun with the intent of killing his wife, although he instead killed someone else in the process. Both the man and his wife insisted, however, that they thought the gun was unloaded. The old guy made a regular practice of waving the always-empty shotgun in their arguments, and both said they were stunned the weapon was loaded. According to the law, then, the death of Opus was an accident because the gun was not intentionally loaded.

The investigation, however, took an even stranger twist when an eyewitness said that he'd seen the couple's son loading the shotgun about six weeks before the fatal accident. The old woman had cut off her son's financial support, and knowing his father's habit of brandishing the gun during arguments, the son loaded the gun, hoping that his father would kill his mother. Then, according to his plan, his father would spend the rest of his life in prison, and the family's money would belong to the son. Ronald Opus's death, therefore, became a case of murder at the hands of the couple's son.

Even at this point the story isn't over. Investigators found that the couple's son had become increasingly despondent over his loss of income and the apparent failure of his plan to have his father murder his mother. This led him to jump off a ten-story building on March 23, 1994, only to be killed by a shotgun blast as he fell past a ninth-story window. In short, Ronald Opus murdered himself—and the medical examiner closed the case as a suicide.[1]

I'm trying to be sensitive to what must have been a difficult day for that family, but Ronald Opus sure went to a lot of trouble to shoot himself in the head!

On the other hand, I've seen a lot of Christians go to an enormous amount of trouble to shoot themselves, spiritually speaking, in the foot. I've had a great deal of experience doing that myself.

On the night before his death, Jesus used a plant to drive home a point. That point? We don't have to continually hurt ourselves in our Christian walk!

Imagine you are walking toward the Garden of Gethsemane, listening. Jesus is breathing a little hard; for he's just walked down the steep path from the city into the Kidron Valley, alongside a dry creek bed, and has begun climbing the first incline of the Mount of Olives. Jesus had often come to this quiet place. All around these twelve men, vines and plants were waiting to be harvested. Glancing toward the plants, Jesus gives us the key for *not* hurting ourselves.

> I am the true vine, and my Father is the gardener. He cuts off every branch in me that bears no fruit, while every branch that does bear fruit he prunes so that it will be even more fruitful. You are already clean because of the word I have spoken to you. Remain in me, and I will remain in you. No branch can bear fruit by itself; it must remain in the vine. Neither can you bear fruit unless you remain in me.
>
> I am the vine; you are the branches. If a man remains in me and I in him, he will bear much fruit; apart from me you can do nothing. If anyone does not remain in me, he is like a branch that is thrown away and withers; such branches are picked up, thrown into the fire and burned. If you remain in

me and my words remain in you, ask whatever you wish,
and it will be given you. This is to my Father's glory, that you
bear much fruit, showing yourselves to be my disciples.

—John 15:1–8

Jesus said to these men, who were on the verge of a nightmare,
"Stay on the vine. Don't leave. Don't do things that will make you
unfruitful. Stay right here, inside this relationship."

Do we overlook this instruction?

Instead of staying in the vine, some Christians watch movies
that dishonor Christ. Some make excuses while on the way to a
party that they know would be displeasing to Christ. Some repeatedly give in to their addictions. Some fill their minds with
ungodly thoughts, music, and photographs. Some disregard
sexual discipline when they leave town alone for a business meeting. Some do well for a few days, but then ignore the relationship
for an afternoon, intentionally embracing an action they know
to be wrong.

In short, Christians who don't stay on the vine, who don't main-
tain a vibrant relationship with Christ, who go out of their way to
enjoy a temptation, are loading the gun that blasts them on the
way down from the willful leap into sin. The disasters that follow
shouldn't come as surprises.

We've all made choices that have, in some measure, taken us
out of this vine, the relationship with Christ.

Please, though, do not read into these words an ability for a
Christian to do something so sinful that it would take him or her
out of the promise of salvation. Jesus has encased all of this last
teaching inside the promises of blessings, peace, and joy. Those
rewards are the things that can be lost if we intentionally attach
ourselves to sin, but our home in heaven is secure, even if we
prove unwise and unfaithful for a season.

If heaven could be lost by what Jesus is saying here, he wouldn't have told the story of the prodigal son, who received his father's welcome upon arriving home and who was *never disowned* by his father. If heaven could be lost by not standing for Jesus in a tough time, then all of the disciples just got kicked out of heaven. They, after all, spent the weekend after Jesus' crucifixion in unparalleled denial. If this passage is about losing your salvation, Jesus wouldn't have said what he did about eternal security. His words, uttered before that last Passover, are recorded by John:

> My sheep listen to my voice; I know them, and they follow me. I give them eternal life, and they shall never perish; no one can snatch them out of my hand. My Father, who has given them to me, is greater than all; no one can snatch them out of my Father's hand. I and the Father are one.
>
> —John 10:27–30

No, once a person is covered by the blood of Christ, nothing— not even a Christian's foolish choices—will uncover him or her. Regardless, most Christians find themselves separated from the vine at some point in their walk with Christ. Most of us wind up out there with the miserable prodigal, foolishly eating gnawed-over corn cobs with the pigs. And no one inflicts that kind of pain upon us—except us.

That's why the last words of Jesus were so passionate about our staying in a right fellowship with him. He doesn't want us to hurt ourselves. He doesn't want us to squander our joy in a far country with the prodigal. He doesn't want us to cut ourselves off from the vine.

Nevertheless, many, many Christians make choices that remove them from their healthy walk with Christ. They take themselves away from the vine. And, to be frank, that's why some Christians never find the blessings, never find the peace, and never find the joy that Jesus promises here.

These blessings can still be found by obeying the commands of Christ. Walking toward the garden, he issued several important commands in rapid succession:

> Remain in me, and I will remain in you.
>
> —John 15:4a

> This is to my Father's glory, that you bear much fruit, showing yourselves to be my disciples.
>
> —John 15:8

> As the Father has loved me, so have I loved you. Now remain in my love.
>
> —John 15:9

> My command is this: Love each other as I have loved you.
>
> —John 15:12

> You did not choose me, but I chose you and appointed you to go and bear fruit—fruit that will last.
>
> —John 15:16a

> This is my command: Love each other.
>
> —John 15:17

Do those things, follow those commands, and you'll be in the vine. You won't be perfect, but you'll be in the vine.

Remain in Christ. Get into Bible study, and stay in it. Learn all you can. Stay in fellowship with other Christians, practicing love on each other. As you do these things, bear fruit. Tell others about what Christ has done for you and bring them into the kingdom. Give of your resources—time, talents, and treasures—to build up the body of Christ. Find your place of service, and serve well.

These activities are both mundane and fulfilling. But following these commands of Jesus places you in a lifestyle of joy, enjoying the kind of laughter that transcends all circumstances. It's a life that leads us, in fact, to what may be the greatest of the three promises.

> As the Father has loved me, so have I loved you. Now remain in my love. If you obey my commands, you will remain in my love, just as I have obeyed my Father's commands and remain in his love. *I have told you this so that my joy may be in you and that your joy may be complete.* My command is this: Love each other as I have loved you. Greater love has no one than this, that he lay down his life for his friends. You are my friends if you do what I command. I no longer call you servants, because a servant does not know his master's business. Instead, I have called you friends, for everything that I learned from my Father I have made known to you. You did not choose me, but I chose you and appointed you to go and bear fruit—fruit that will last. Then the Father will give you whatever you ask in my name. This is my command: Love each other.
>
> —John 15:9–17

I'm embarrassed to use this illustration. I have a grapevine in my backyard, but I harvest from the vines of friends or family. My grapevine squats along the ground, desperately seeking water and a place to grow. It can't find an arbor because I haven't built one. It produces no harvest because I neither prune, water, nor fertilize my grapevine. Last year, half a dozen green grapes appeared, but a bird took them all.

I have no doubt as to why my vine is so inferior to the vines of my family and friends. They take care of their grapevines all year long. They prune in the winter, shore up the arbor in the spring, prune again in early summer, add the right fertilizer at the right time, water abundantly in the dry seasons, and protect the harvest from the birds.

They have so many grapes that they have to share the harvest. They store jars of jelly for the winter and eat their fill at fall harvest, right there at the arbor.

I don't put any effort into my vine, and it doesn't bear fruit. My friends and family nurture their vines and have fruit to spare.

In a similar way, doesn't it make sense that if a Christian puts no effort into her walk with Christ, she isn't going to see the reward? If a Christian doesn't know his Bible, how can he rest upon the verses of comfort or of promise? If a Christian hasn't practiced praying, how will she know how to talk with God during times of crisis? If the Christian family hasn't found a church home, how will they know the benefit of enjoying Christian friends?

The careless Christian squats along the backyard of life, barely growing, and producing nothing but a brief delight for the birds. On the other hand, Christians who make the commitment to learn the Bible's message have a treasure chest of wealth at their disposal. Christians who pray every day have a rich walk with the Lord. They see prayers answered. They have shared their faith with others, sometimes without even being aware of it, and their lives are filled with a joy that overcomes all circumstances. It's a full joy, a complete joy, the culmination of the abundant life that Jesus offered.

Has a greater offer ever been made to any human being? Jesus said, "If you remain in me, and my words remain in you, ask *whatever you wish,* and it will be given you" (John 15:7).

So many people who consider becoming Christians stop short when they think of what they'll have to give up. They often point to the usual list—drunkenness, sexual sins, profanity, materialism—things that have brought them pleasure in the past. How I wish that I could show them what's being offered by Christ. Their desire to hang onto their old lives makes me think of a really dumb teenager who keeps saying, "No, I'd rather not have the bright, shiny sports car because I really like my bicycle."

So how do we stay on the vine? How do we connect with this illustration that Jesus used? Once again, it's simple—but not necessarily easy. Obey the commands of Jesus. Jesus focuses on our loving one another. He tells us to lay down our lives for others, to show them our greatest love. Jesus did that on the cross. We'll do it in smaller ways. Serve one another. Wash some feet. Do something that's really hard, and dirty, and distasteful. But do it with the right motive. Do it not for yourself, but for the Father's glory. See if you can do it anonymously.

Jesus emphasized that it is important for us to learn, to spend a lifetime in discipleship. In the heart of the passage above, he said, "Everything that I learned from my Father I have made known to you" (John 15:15b).

Finally, Jesus emphasized the importance of sharing the gospel with anyone who will listen. This is so important that Jesus started his walk to the garden with a warning: "He [the Father] cuts off every branch in me that bears no fruit" (John 15:2). In other words, some Christians live moral lives and stay out of the wrong thoughts, but because they refuse to share the gospel, they never benefit from the blessings, joy, or peace that Jesus offered.

If you make a habit of sharing the gospel, you'll get better at it. Part of the process of improving, however, may not be pleasant. According to the "cutting-back" illustration that Jesus used, the Father will prune you to make you more fruitful. He'll allow some pain in your life to produce more fruit.

In 1995, the sports world watched baseball legend Mickey Mantle die. He had been one of the greatest players that baseball had ever seen, playing for one of the greatest teams of the twentieth century, the New York Yankees. In 1995, however, Mantle was losing his battle with alcoholism and cancer. His hard lifestyle had been no secret from the fans, the media, or his teammates. His teammates could always count on Mantle for some wild times.

Another great player for the Yankees during Mantle's years was third baseman Bobby Richardson. Exhibiting quite the opposite lifestyle, the quiet Richardson was dubbed by Mantle as "Milk Drinker." "Hey, Milk Drinker," Mantle recalled asking Richardson. "Want to join us for cards?" The ragging about Richardson's clean-cut, Christian life continued throughout the playing careers of both men. It was fun for Mantle and tough on Richardson. You might say that the pain in the locker room was part of Richardson's "pruning." Even so, a deep friendship developed between the two players. And when Mantle learned, forty years later, that he was desperately ill because of his alcoholism, it wasn't his drinking buddies whom he called—it was Milk Drinker.

"Pray for me," Mantle asked, when he called Richardson from his hospital room. And later, when he became so seriously ill and had only a short time to live, Mantle asked Richardson to visit him. Richardson came, and there on the front page of *The New York Times* sports section was an incredible quote.

"Bobby," Mantle was quoted as saying when the two met face to face, "I just wanted you to know that I've accepted Jesus Christ as my Savior."

What a miracle! And yet it was more than four decades in the making. For Richardson, it was forty years of waiting.

Are you interested in bearing fruit with your life? Plant the seeds. Water, cultivate, and prune. Stay in the vine of Christ, and simply be faithful. Your harvest will come—perhaps in forty minutes, perhaps in forty years.

In the meantime, bear fruit.

Eleven

This Is Going to Be Tough

Years ago, in the "B.C." era—that's "Before Children"—my wife and I volunteered to help get Christmas ready for a young family member.

This little girl was into dolls, and the number one item on her wish list was something called a "Malibu Barbie Dream Vacation Van." Her mother, my wife's aunt, asked if I'd assemble the van on Christmas Eve.

"Why not?" I said, and we were handed a large box of unassembled Barbie transportation. I tipped the box and *hundreds* of parts spilled out of the carton. Whatever delusions I had about the quick assembly of this Christmas gift vanished. The shell of the van was stuffed with tiny plastic bags full of accessories. Pages of tiny stickers were supposed to transform the bland, pink vehicle into the state-of-the-art Dream Vacation Van pictured on the box. The instruction manual rivaled the IRS tax code in complexity.

"Where did all of these parts come from?" I asked my wife. She was already thumbing through the manual, aware that our Christmas Eve was about to be dominated by Malibu Barbie's sinister smile.

Before that long night was over, I vowed that my children would have nothing to do with anything Barbie. Naturally, we had three daughters and they owned practically *everything* Barbie's manufacturer could produce, as fast as the hundreds of tiny parts could be packed into colorful cartons.

If life has ever handed you a box of trouble, you can understand what Jesus said on the last night of his earthly existence. And if you've ever been confused by life's instruction book, you can relate to this scene. If the worst trouble you've ever seen is assembling a Christmas toy, you have no need for this chapter. More than likely, however, you've seen some tough times or you sense them lurking not far away.

This entire book is based on a simple premise: Jesus promised great blessings to those who would follow him, blessings that would include such a richness of peace and joy that laughter would be a part of every Christian's daily life. Jesus, however, made one more promise: As you laugh your way through life, the world might not laugh with you. In fact, the world may hate you. That's the unexpected trouble in the box.

Jesus led eleven disciples away from the Upper Room and toward the Garden of Gethsemane. They walked through the narrow streets, slipping through one of Jerusalem's stone gates and into the darkness. As they walked, Jesus wasted no time. He was teaching his last lesson before the cross.

Perhaps he spotted a pair of Roman guards, armed with swords and read to nail any would-be messiah to a cross. Maybe Jesus saw a Jewish Pharisee, rushing toward a hastily called meeting at Caiaphas's quarters. Judas would be there by now, working out the final details of history's greatest betrayal.

Perhaps Jesus simply looked into the future and saw the problems for people who took on the name *Christian*. As you develop a lifestyle of joy, that same laughter of your soul might be repulsive to people around you.

Jesus begins with a shocking statement: "If the world *hates* you . . ." At that moment, he had the full attention of the skittish disciples and all others who would ever find trouble when they expected joy.

> If the world hates you, keep in mind that it hated me first. If you belonged to the world, it would love you as its own. As it is, you do not belong to the world, but I have chosen you out of the world. That is why the world hates you. Remember the words I spoke to you: "No servant is greater than his master." If they persecuted me, they will persecute you also. If they obeyed my teaching, they will obey yours also. They will treat you this way because of my name, for they do not know the One who sent me. If I had not come and spoken to them, they would not be guilty of sin. Now, however, they have no excuse for their sin. He who hates me hates my Father as well. If I had not done among them what no one else did, they would not be guilty of sin. But now they have seen these miracles, and yet they have hated both me and my Father. But this is to fulfill what is written in their Law: "They hated me without reason."
>
> —John 15:18–25

As we read the words, we nod our heads and agree that there are times when the world hates us. We think of harsh words, or being shunned, or sharp barbs thrown at us from people who don't have the same values. Perhaps we think of missionaries who are being threatened in various locations all over the world.

Think how Jesus was hated. He had been chased for months

by the very religious leaders who prayed every day that God would send the Christ. They had sought to trap him with words, and now they were gathering up weapons for a search through the darkness, hoping to display his bloody frame on a cross.

The chase had been tiring for Jesus. His words give insight as to how tired he had become: "But this is to fulfill what is written in their Law: 'They hated me without reason'" (John 15:25).

Jesus was quoting Scripture. The original statements are in two places—Psalms 35 and 69. Both passages are psalms of David, and they appear in an exhausted man's prayer to God for relief from enemies who hate him. Jesus so related to the words that he referred to them while on the run with his disciples. He drew on them from memory in this hour. Let the implication soak in— Jesus felt like a hated man.

Read the phrases below that David used hundreds of years before the birth of Jesus. Read them aloud, and listen to the words with an eye toward Jesus, who knew far in advance that one day he'd be chased by enemies.

> Contend, O Lord, with those who contend with me;
>   fight against those who fight against me. . . .
> May those who seek my life
>   be disgraced and put to shame;
>   may those who plot my ruin
>   be turned back in dismay. . . .
> Since they hid their net for me without cause
>   and without cause dug a pit for me,
>   may ruin overtake them by surprise—
>   may the net they hid entangle them,
>   may they fall into the pit, to their ruin. . . .
> Ruthless witnesses come forward;
>   they question me on things I know nothing about.
> They repay me evil for good

and leave my soul forlorn. . . .
Let not those gloat over me
   who are my enemies without cause;
   let not *those who hate me without reason*
   maliciously wink the eye.

—Psalm 35:1–19

Save me, O God,
   for the waters have come up to my neck.
I sink in the miry depths,
   where there is no foothold.
I have come into the deep waters;
   the floods engulf me.
I am worn out calling for help;
   my throat is parched.
My eyes fail,
   looking for my God.
Those who hate me without reason
   outnumber the hairs of my head;
   many are my enemies without cause,
   those who seek to destroy me.
I am forced to restore
   what I did not steal. . . .
You know how I am scorned, disgraced and shamed;
   all my enemies are before you.
Scorn has broken my heart
   and has left me helpless;
I looked for sympathy, but there was none,
   for comforters, but I found none.
They put gall in my food
   and gave me vinegar for my thirst.

—Psalm 69:1–21

"If the world hates you," Jesus says to us, "please realize that it hated me first. That's part of the price tag for receiving the blessings I have to offer. People around you might not jump for joy when you're filled with joy. When you have peace, someone might try to make you miserable just to have company. When you have blessings, nonbelievers might passionately try to do you harm."

Christians who are filled with the abundant life will stand out in their community. The world will hate you because the world hates the light. The light by its very nature exposes the darkness. If you shine a flashlight into your attic, you see a lot of dust. If you turn on a shop light under the hood of an old car, you'll see a lot of grime. If you speak out against abortion clinics, strip clubs, or a host of other ungodly practices, the criticism will come. It might come from inside your own family, inside your circle of close friends, or even from voices in your community.

As Christians in America speak out in larger numbers and with louder voices, the objections come. Sometimes the criticism is as mild as being given a label—"Religious Right," "fundamentalists," and "religious extremists." Sometimes the attacks are personal and hateful. Sometimes elected officials who are committed Christians face attacks from the media for conducting office devotions or prayer meetings or for applying biblical standards to their decisions at work.

The Internet teems with attacks on Christians who dare to speak out against ungodly practices. Enter the name of any Christian leader on a search engine and you'll come across web sites that spew some of the most vicious personal attacks found anywhere.

American media seem to have developed a "politically correct" mind-set that doesn't allow for Christian elected leaders to hold devotions with their staff or for Christian cartoonists to deliver the gospel message through the Sunday comic pages. The pressure exerted against Christians who don't agree to practice a "silent faith" can be tremendous.

Across the world, some international governments are creating and enforcing laws that are meant to silence Christians who speak out on moral or evangelical issues. Some missionaries operate under a code of secrecy to protect their lives. Some Christians endure attacks from a painfully personal and private corner—the family.

Reading the words of Jesus on his last night of life, it's easy to think that he was talking directly to us:

> All this I have told you so that you will not go astray. They will put you out of the synagogue; in fact, a time is coming when anyone who kills you will think he is offering a service to God. They will do such things because they have not known the Father or me. I have told you this, so that when the time comes you will remember that I warned you. I did not tell you this at first because I was with you.
>
> —John 16:1–4

In short, the pain won't become personal until it happens to you. When a relative pokes fun at your decision to follow Christ, when a friend laughs at your stand on a moral issue, or when a business associate ridicules your belief in God, the pain is as real as a dog bite. And although you know that the bite isn't deadly, it surely does hurt. Sometimes, the pain comes from inside the church, the very place that should be a haven from hatred. If that's been true in your life, remember that almost all of Jesus' trouble came from people in his "church."

Enough of the pain. Where does the laughter come into play?

The laughter never left. Jesus simply gave us a very real, very serious warning that in the midst of our blessings, joy, and peace, there will be tough times. The peace will come in three ways.

First, Jesus promised to send the Holy Spirit, the One he called the *Counselor:*

When the Counselor comes, whom I will send to you from
the Father, the Spirit of truth who goes out from the Father,
he will testify about me. And you also must testify, for you
have been with me from the beginning.

—John 15:26–27

The Greek word for *counselor* is *parakletos,* a term that meant
"helper." A counselor would come alongside you when you
needed assistance. In particular, a lawyer who defended you in
an ancient courtroom would be referred to as your *parakletos.*
You wouldn't have to testify to your own character because the
parakletos who stands beside you would do it for you. Jesus did
not leave us alone in a world that he promised would hate us. He
told the apostles that God would soon be sending a *parakletos*
like the world had never seen.

Christians have a second reason to experience peace in the
midst of tough times. Simply put, they know how it will be in the
end. For the disciples, this gloomy prediction of trouble was off-
set by Jesus' promise that their "grief will turn to joy" (John 16:20).
Jesus used the illustration of a woman in labor finally giving birth
to a precious child. Most of the disciples understood that illustration. At least some of them were married, and perhaps they
had witnessed the birth of their own children. If so, they had seen
their wives forget the anguish of delivery as soon as they nursed
the baby.

On the Passover evening in question, Jesus told his disciples
that the experience of the next few days would be like a woman
giving birth. First, death will come—in hours, on the cross—and
they would mourn as they had never mourned before. In a short
time, however, they would see Jesus again, and their joy would
be wild and unrestrained. While they would never forget the cross,
the pain of the weekend would give way to a torrent of joy. It would
be the joy, not the pain, that would dominate their lives.

In the same way, disciplined Christians today have developed a positive, long-range view of life. They might have a few tough times along the way, but the ending of the story is already written. The promise at the end of this physical life of ours is eternal life and all that God has planned for us in eternity. And eternity always makes life on earth look mighty brief.

Finally, Christians have peace because the Holy Spirit will constantly and consistently guide us into truth. No matter what the current public opinion polls say, no matter how popular or unpopular the Bible's stand on issues might be, the Holy Spirit, the One who stands beside you, will help you see the truth. And there is something wonderfully peaceful about knowing the truth.

> Now I am going to him who sent me, yet none of you asks me, "Where are you going?" Because I have said these things, you are filled with grief. But I tell you the truth: It is for your good that I am going away. Unless I go away, the Counselor will not come to you; but if I go, I will send him to you. When he comes, he will convict the world of guilt in regard to sin and righteousness and judgment: in regard to sin, because men do not believe in me; in regard to righteousness, because I am going to the Father, where you can see me no longer; and in regard to judgment, because the prince of this world now stands condemned.
>
> I have much more to say to you, more than you can now bear. But when he, the Spirit of truth, comes, he will guide you into all truth. He will not speak on his own; he will speak only what he hears, and he will tell you what is yet to come. He will bring glory to me by taking from what is mine and making it known to you. All that belongs to the Father is mine. That is why I said the Spirit will take from what is mine and make it known to you.
>
> —John 16:5–15

You've got good reason to feel peaceful, even in the midst of tough times. You've got the comforting presence of the Holy Spirit, you know the end of the story, and you have opportunity to know the truth, no matter what seemingly contradictory messages swirl around you. It's a very peaceful position.

Pastor Eric S. Ritz, of Easton, Pennsylvania, told of some modern-day treasure hunters off the New Jersey coastline. Armed with sophisticated equipment, their ships had found an old wreck, but they hadn't been able to locate the ancient treasure for days. None of their high-tech tools could find the large stash of gold that they had expected.

Suddenly, the treasure was found. Actually, the treasure gave itself up. After years of being under great water pressure, the outer coating on the treasure chest finally gave way, yielding all that was buried inside. The hinges of the great chest tore loose, the box burst, the lid floated off, and the riches were exposed for the fortunate underwater explorers.

There's a treasure of blessings, peace, and joy available, and many Christians collect only a few coins that are scattered about the chest. In good times, in times of comfort, that's all that you can really have. A coin of joy here, a coin of peace there. It's a blessing, sure, but a small one.

In time, however, there will come seasons of pressure, great and relentless pressure. You'll have trouble, and it might seem that the world hates you. When that happens, hold on. Look again in a familiar place. Don't miss the golden opportunity. It might be *only when the pressure overwhelms you* that the lid on the blessings breaks loose and God's richest treasures are exposed. When that happens, you can take as much of God's joy and peace as you can hold.

Twelve

Laughter at a Funeral

One Friday night not long ago was so exciting that I had trouble getting to sleep. The reason for the excitement? I had just watched a funeral on television.

You're probably thinking, If this man gets excited over a funeral, he doesn't have much of a life!

Let me explain. Years ago, I was a sports writer. I dearly loved my job, especially when it took me to the golf course. Covering golf (and playing a little along the way) was my passion. And each spring my job actually paid me to go to Augusta. If you're into golf, you're already visualizing the Georgia azaleas in full bloom, the dogwoods putting on a show of color, and the manicured grass of Augusta National shimmering like polished emerald. They play the Masters in Augusta each spring, and that's where I met several famous golfers.

I interviewed a lot of them. Nicklaus, Palmer, Player, Watson, Ballesteros, Norman. I was there the day that Nicklaus won the title at age forty-six. Ditto when Mize chipped in to beat Norman. I saw Langer and Lyle take home green jackets, the coats that go to the champions.

Each spring one golfer always appeared to be in full bloom.

That golfer was Payne Stewart. He wore a distinctive outfit: knickers and long socks, matching gold-tipped and polished shoes, a flawless shirt, and a dapper Tam o' Shanter to cap it off. The clothes were Stewart's trademark, and he was quickly recognized by millions of people by both his clothing and his trophies. He won two U.S. Opens and a host of other titles. He was a regular on the Ryder Cup, and his easy-going nature made him a hit with fans and fellow pros alike.

And suddenly, he was gone. A tragedy unfolded in the air, and our nation watched it on CNN. His plane was a ghost plane, apparently deprived of oxygen and any hope of rescue, it crashed long after everyone aboard was dead. And the nation mourned. The only golfer that even nongolfers could recognize was dead. The media started in on the stories.

They told of his beautiful Australian wife and two young children. They told of his love for fishing and his passion for humor. They reported on his rapid climb to stardom, his struggle with his swing in the middle years, and his return to top form. The networks continually replayed his dramatic putt on the seventy-second hole that won the 1999 U.S. Open, the last national championship of the twentieth century. The networks tried to tell every single angle of the story.

That's why they eventually began telling about Payne Stewart's faith. Stewart had been profoundly affected by the faith of other players and individuals around him. Paul Azinger's battle with cancer had been strengthened by his own Christian faith, and Stewart was intrigued. About the same time, his children began attending a Christian school in Orlando. Both Stewart and his wife renewed their walk with Christ. As his faith blossomed,

Stewart began to change. In the last two years of his life, he became more generous with his time at home, his attention to others, and with his money. He found contentment. He found joy.

Stewart hadn't been shy about his new-found source of strength. After the drama of the '99 U.S. Open, friends thought that the tears in his eyes were from the thrill of a great golfing conquest. Stewart corrected them: "I just want everyone to know, it's Jesus that has done this for me. It's Jesus that has changed my life."[1]

Stewart's memorial service was a celebration service. Tears were plentiful, but there was laughter, too. Fellow golfers—including Azinger—talked openly about Payne's faith in Jesus Christ. Pastors talked of his rapid growth through discipleship. His wife talked of his changed heart. The plan of salvation was illustrated in plain, golfers' language, and every major network covered the service. Outside the church where the service was held, thirty-two television trucks beamed the pictures to satellites and waiting televisions. Thirty-two! Every major newspaper in America covered the events of the week and the newfound peace that Payne Stewart had found in Jesus.

When the cameras panned the crowd, I picked out the golfers who were believers. For years, many of them had made no secret of their faith in Christ.

They wept. Christians or not, it hurt to lose a friend. But they also laughed. Then they cried. Then they smiled. In short, for two hours, the world watched as Christian golfers grieved. What they saw was different than simple grief. This was grief with hope. There's a profound difference between grief alone and grief with hope.

Maybe that's how Jesus was able to talk so openly about his death, how he was able to combine statements about his own death with profound statements about joy. As you read the Bible's account of the life of Jesus, you get the feeling that Jesus wanted to be more open and more plainspoken about his upcoming death. Only the disciples' fears kept him from saying more.

Nevertheless, Jesus spoke plainly about his future. One of those occasions happened just weeks before the last night of his earthly life:

> They were on their way up to Jerusalem, with Jesus leading the way, and the disciples were astonished, while *those who followed were afraid*. Again he took the Twelve aside and told them what was going to happen to him. "We are going up to Jerusalem," he said, "and the Son of Man will be betrayed to the chief priests and teachers of the law. They will condemn him to death and will hand him over to the Gentiles, who will mock him and spit on him, flog him and kill him. Three days later he will rise."
>
> —Mark 10:32–34

On that night, Jesus kept making references to his approaching death, circling around this distressing news, closing in on the subject that the disciples equated with incredible pain.

Please note this important part of the Scripture: Jesus did not discount the pain of the disciples. There is nothing funny about death, nothing funny about the loss of a loved one. Jesus knew this personally because he had already lived through the deaths of several people whom he loved. His own stepfather, for instance, isn't mentioned during his adult life. Most scholars speculate that Joseph's absence indicates he had died. If so, Joseph's death must have hurt Jesus deeply. When Lazarus died, Jesus wept openly. As his own death approached, Jesus was stressed as he'd never been stressed before. Death is, undeniably, painful to face.

Nevertheless, Jesus was trying to communicate a reason for joy even at funerals. He began speaking very plainly to the eleven men who listened to his last teaching:

"In a little while you will see me no more, and then after a little while you will see me."

Some of his disciples said to one another, "What does he mean by saying, 'In a little while you will see me no more, and then after a little while you will see me,' and 'Because I am going to the Father'?" They kept asking, "What does he mean by 'a little while'? We don't understand what he is saying."

Jesus saw that they wanted to ask him about this, so he said to them, "Are you asking one another what I meant when I said, 'In a little while you will see me no more, and then after a little while you will see me'? I tell you the truth, you will weep and mourn while the world rejoices. You will grieve, but your grief will turn to joy. A woman giving birth to a child has pain because her time has come; but when her baby is born she forgets the anguish because of her joy that a child is born into the world. So with you: *Now is your time of grief,* but I will see you again and *you will rejoice, and no one will take away your joy.* In that day you will no longer ask me anything. I tell you the truth, my Father will give you whatever you ask in my name. Until now you have not asked for anything in my name. Ask and you will receive, and your joy will be complete."

—John 16:16–24

I'm familiar with childbirth only from the vantage point of an expectant father. My wife and I have gone through labor pains together three times. Actually, she went through the pain, and I drove the car. Nevertheless, I was by her side and remember those agonizing hours of physical torment.

Actually, I have to force myself to remember the pain. Every time I try to remember the labor pains, I skip forward to the joy of holding a baby. Every time I try to reflect upon the intense agony, I relive the phone calls after each birth to family and friends.

"It's a girl!"

"It's another girl!"

"It's yet another girl!"

Spread over a ten-year period, the announcement never lost its thrill. Not one time did we ever call friends and say, "We just had several hours of pain—it was horrible!"

No, we hardly mentioned to anyone the pain before the birth. To be sure, neither the labor nor the birth trauma was easy or short. The joy of a baby, however, overwhelmed all other emotions.

Jesus used that same illustration with men who had seen it for themselves: "A woman giving birth to a child has pain because her time has come; but when her baby is born she forgets the anguish because of her joy that a child is born into the world. So [it is] with you . . ." (John 16:21–22a).

Could the disciples believe that joy would so overwhelm their emotions that they would forget the anguish of Calvary?

It happened.

A survey of the Gospels shows that all of the Bible's historians include a great deal of information about the arrest, trial, and crucifixion of Jesus. In fact, there are more than twice as many words about the events surrounding the Crucifixion than about the Resurrection. The passion contained in the words of the Resurrection, however, is undeniable. Exclamation points litter John's record of the Resurrection.

John records the screams of Mary. According to his account in John 20, a weeping Mary turned toward the living, resurrected Jesus and cried out, "Rabboni!" At the end of a run, she shouts, breathless, to the disciples, "I have seen the Lord!" Thomas gets special attention in John's gospel. When the doubter finally sees Jesus a week after the others, he falls on his knees and says, "My

Lord and my God!" The Bible also records Peter's sprint through the waters of the Sea of Galilee, while John himself remembers pulling in one last miraculous catch of fish.

Luke, the historian, found two men who, after the Resurrection, ran several miles back to Jerusalem with the news that they had walked with Jesus on the road to Emmaus. While they were still describing their encounter to those in Jerusalem, Jesus appeared in their midst, stunning them and filling them with a joy never before experienced. The last words of Luke's account—which covers an event that happened six weeks after the Emmaus encounter—are packed with joy.

> When he had led them out to the vicinity of Bethany, he lifted up his hands and blessed them. While he was blessing them, he left them and was taken up into heaven. Then they worshiped him and returned to Jerusalem with great joy. And they stayed continually at the temple, praising God.
>
> —Luke 24:50–53

Matthew ends his account of the Resurrection with what must have been the most comforting promise he had ever heard. He would never again have to endure the absence of Jesus. "And surely," Jesus said, "I am with you always, to the very end of the age" (Matt. 28:20b).

We know that the eyewitnesses were filled with joy because of the Resurrection. They saw it, and they felt it; they touched Jesus, and they worshiped at his feet.

Is there any hope that we can have that same joy of personally experiencing Jesus' resurrection? Jesus said there is. In fact, he spelled out the way—the way people can know that they will spend eternal life in heaven, the way that they can turn their own funerals into times of God-given laughter: "I tell you the truth," he said, "whoever hears my word and believes him who sent me has eternal life and will not be condemned; he has crossed over from death to life" (John 5:24).

Read it again. As soon as a person believes in Jesus as the Son of God, the Messiah, the Christ, the One sent to pay the price for the sin of those who would accept the gift, *at that moment* there is a passing over from death to life. Instead of hopelessness in the face of death, hope gives way to certainty. Instead of something to fear, death becomes the doorway to heaven. Instead of paralyzing pain, comfort arrives in knowing that the future is secure.

Could you really laugh at the thought of your own funeral?

Let's go over the basics, one more time. Throughout his final teachings, Jesus emphasized three major commands. First, we are to remain in him. From a practical standpoint, we can "remain" in Christ through Bible study, prayer, and fellowship with other believers. Second, we are to share our faith consistently and compassionately as we go through life. That's bearing fruit. Third, through it all, we are to love others the way Jesus loves us. If we do all three of these things, and keep doing them, we'll *eventually* develop a joy so complete that we can find joy even at a funeral.

I'd like to share one more story with you—one that happened a long way from the Augusta National and the spotlights of national television. Instead of millions, only a handful of people saw it happen. Instead of television reporters, only a few observed what took place. Here's how it happened.

Four years into my ministry, I became acquainted with a woman from our community who had been hospitalized. She was terminally ill with cancer, and she seemed to welcome my visits, even though we'd never met before. At least one of her two daughters, however, was always with her, and the daughters gave cold shoulders to a preacher's company. These were rough folks from a rough area of the county. A lot of drinking, shooting, fighting, and who knows what else went on in this lady's neck of the woods. Our conversations tended to be short and to the point.

"Mrs. Jackson," I asked on one visit, "are you a member of a church?"

"No."

"Are you a Christian?"

"No, can't say that I am."

Sharing Christ with this dying woman became a passion for me. Over the next two weeks, I saw her every time I made hospital visits. At least one of the daughters was always there, however, guarding against conversations of spiritual substance. It seemed very strange, and it was very frustrating.

One Thursday, on my way to an appointment in another town, I stopped at the hospital to see a church member. There wasn't time for much of a visit, and by the time I'd seen the church member, I was already running late. Still, something inside me said, "See Mrs. Jackson. *Now.*"

When I got to her room neither daughter was there.

In a few moments, I was sharing the plan of salvation with Mrs. Jackson. She listened closely. She was sitting up, which was different from the other visits, and she seemed very alert. We had moved so quickly, I was afraid that it had been *too* quickly.

"I don't want you to think I'm pushing you to make this decision," I told her. "I don't want you to pray a prayer to accept Christ just so this preacher will leave you alone. So I'll tell you what. I'll leave, you can think about it, and I'll check back with you tomorrow."

I stood up to leave, and she grabbed my sleeve. She had a lot of strength in those hands, and she pulled hard.

"Sit down," she said firmly. "I want to say that prayer."

I sat down, she prayed, and the angels rejoiced.

The next day, I was at that hospital again. I slipped in to see Mrs. Jackson and saw something that had been missing in all of my earlier visits. Mrs. Jackson was smiling. She was beaming! No television or radio was on, and no visitors were in the room. All by herself, Mrs. Jackson was wearing the kind of smile she had never known before. She had been a believer for only twenty-four hours, but she already knew the joy. On this visit, we laughed together as brother and sister in Christ.

One week later, she was dead.

As the funeral approached, I realized that no one knew the story. I was unable to locate the preacher who was to conduct the funeral until the day of the service. There, only thirty minutes before the funeral sermon, I told him the story. It seemed hard for him to believe, because he knew this family. He knew their roughness. He knew their hopelessness, their sin, their attitude. He didn't like having been thrust into their sordid affairs. But he was intrigued by my story and by Mrs. Jackson's smile.

The funeral started, and he mumbled through the first five minutes or so. Both daughters cried so loudly that it was hard to hear anything over their wails. Not many folks were in the chapel, mainly just family, a few friends, and me, a young Baptist pastor, praying in the back row.

Suddenly, the Spirit of God struck that old preacher and he got real. *Very* real. He announced to a shocked family that the woman in the casket had accepted Christ in her hospital room just a week earlier. She had smiled and found the peace that passes all understanding right at the end of her life. There was reason to celebrate, to praise God, to thank God, for a soul saved.

The crying ceased immediately. The daughters were stunned. Then the preacher really got wound up.

"But ain't it a tragedy," he boomed, "that this woman wasted her life? Ain't it a tragedy that she waited until the very end of her life to give her heart to Christ? She could have done so much for the Lord had she given her life to him earlier. But she wasted it."

I think the preacher figured that he'd already blown the honorarium, so he just put the hammer down. He started pointing at people and pointing at the casket.

"And let me tell you girls something," he said. "If you ever want to see your mama again, you'd better get right with God. If you don't, this is the last time you'll ever see her."

At the side of the grave a few minutes later, he drove home the point again.

I couldn't help but laugh. It was the most fun I'd ever had at a funeral. The Devil lost a candidate just at the end of her life, and her family got an earful of what they needed to hear at the service.

Push aside the laughter, though, and look for the joy. Go back to that hospital room, where nothing on the outside had changed. There were still machines and wires connected to the patient. There was still an oxygen tube under her nose. There was still cancer in her body, and it was still hard for her to breathe. But in the midst of all the hopelessness, Mrs. Jackson was smiling. The labor pains of dying had given way to the joy of birth. A new birth. *Her* new birth.

Has it happened to you?

Thirteen

Never Alone

Being alone can be a good thing.
Being alone can be a bad thing.

We all have an inborn desire to be alone once in a while. Children build secret forts and play house beneath beds and behind storage buildings. Early in life we learn to shut the bedroom door, and then we learn to lock it.

We love to curl up with a good book, undisturbed, and enjoy a quiet hour. We cherish sitting on a back porch in a rocking chair, soaking up the silence. It's instinctive. We're designed to benefit from having some time alone.

At least once a year, I make a getaway, taking only a Bible, a book, some writing materials, and my guitar. It's a week set aside for silence, study, and outlining sermons.

How I love that week. How I hate that week.

Children never stay by themselves for very long in their play forts, and we can't read books on quiet evenings forever. Pastors—

at least the ones I know well—can't take the silence for more than a few days, at the very most. We're created to be with people, and in the give and take of life, we've all discovered that companionship is priceless. At every age, in every community, people seek other people.

I love this story Maxie Dunnam tells. An elderly man began to spend a significant amount of time with an elderly woman. Neither had ever married and each had lived alone for many years. Gradually, the old gentleman recognized a real attachment to his lady friend but was shy and afraid to reveal his feelings. After many days of anxiety and fear, he finally mustered up the courage to declare his intentions. He charged over to her home and in a nervous frenzy blurted out, "Let's get married!"

Surprised, she threw up her hands and shouted, "It's a wonderful idea, but who in the world would have us?"

We can have laughter in the very thought of friendship. Joy comes in walking through life together, and we experience blessings simply by being surrounded by family or a circle of friends.

If you have the security of family and friends, it's easy to enjoy solitude. You can enjoy the silence of rocking on the back porch because companionship is only a few steps away, inside the home. You can enjoy time by yourself when a soul mate is only a phone call away. Children play by themselves when they have the security of knowing that they're really not alone. Mom's not far away. Dad's consistently around. Brothers or sisters may be part of the picture. So, for a while, solitude is very good.

But if you're alone because you've been abandoned, it's an entirely different story. If you've been betrayed or forsaken, being alone can be a prison sentence.

Jesus, too, sometimes needed time alone. And on that last Passover evening, he was ready for his place of solitude—under the midnight shadows of the great, ancient walls of old Jerusalem, there in the garden of the oil press at the base of the Mount of

Olives. It probably took Jesus less than twenty minutes to walk from the Upper Room to his favorite hiding place, the kind of place where he would have wanted to hide forever. In the heat of the Middle East, this place was cool. In the noise of overcrowded Jerusalem, it was quiet. After three years of word battles with religious leaders, Jesus must have found something comforting about the setting. The big rocks and the old trees looked solid, unchanging, and true.

In his last bit of teaching, the last morsel he'll give to his disciples, Jesus had some important things to say about life, especially about being alone. By that time, there's not much teaching left. All that remains is a time of prayer, and then Judas will arrive with a mob of soldiers and angry Jewish leaders. Then there will be beatings, a scourging with a whip, a long walk to Calvary, and six hours on a cross. Those horrible hours of torture will begin when his friends leave him—*alone.*

Hear again his last words of instruction to the very men who would abandon him:

> "In that day you will no longer ask me anything. I tell you the truth, my Father will give you whatever you ask in my name. Until now you have not asked for anything in my name. Ask and you will receive, and your joy will be complete.
>
> "Though I have been speaking figuratively, a time is coming when I will no longer use this kind of language but will tell you plainly about my Father. In that day you will ask in my name. I am not saying that I will ask the Father on your behalf. No, the Father himself loves you because you have loved me and have believed that I came from God. I came from the Father and entered the world; now I am leaving the world and going back to the Father."
>
> Then Jesus' disciples said, "Now you are speaking clearly and without figures of speech. Now we can see that you know all

things and that you do not even need to have anyone ask you questions. This makes us believe that you came from God."

"You believe at last!" Jesus answered. "But a time is coming, and has come, when you will be scattered, each to his own home. *You will leave me all alone. Yet I am not alone, for my Father is with me.*

"I have told you these things, so that in me you may have peace. In this world you will have trouble. But take heart! I have overcome the world."

—John 16:23–33

The impact of the words is overwhelming—"You will leave me all alone."

Imagine how it must have been. Imagine how you'd feel if, for example, it's time for your surgery, and your family decides to carry on with their routines rather than be by your side. Or the death of a loved one has devastated you, but no one comes to the funeral. It's just you, a casket, and a big, empty room. Or imagine having terrible chest pains, and having no one around to call 911.

Jesus needed these men to stand beside him, at this hour, in this place. He was alert with the knowledge that the crisis was upon him. The stress Jesus felt was so intense, the Bible tells us that his sweat was like drops of blood falling to the ground. Doctors today speak of capillaries rupturing under intense pressure—the most severe sort of pressure—and mingling with sweat that pops out on the forehead. But while the stress level of the Messiah reached this incredible point, eleven exhausted men slept.

Twice Jesus left his prayers only to find his disciples sleeping. They had promised to be like soldiers, fighting to the death to defend the man whom they considered to be the Son of God. Instead of soldiering, however, they were slumbering. Instead of watching, they were snoring. They weren't alert. They weren't even awake!

Then Jesus went with his disciples to a place called Gethsemane, and he said to them, "Sit here while I go over there and pray." He took Peter and the two sons of Zebedee along with him, and he began to be sorrowful and troubled. Then he said to them, "My soul is overwhelmed with sorrow to the point of death. Stay here and keep watch with me."

Going a little farther, he fell with his face to the ground and prayed, "My Father, if it is possible, may this cup be taken from me. Yet not as I will, but as you will."

Then he returned to his disciples and found them sleeping. "Could you men not keep watch with me for one hour?" he asked Peter. "Watch and pray so that you will not fall into temptation. The spirit is willing, but the body is weak."

He went away a second time and prayed, "My Father, if it is not possible for this cup to be taken away unless I drink it, may your will be done."

When he came back, he again found them sleeping, because their eyes were heavy. So he left them and went away once more and prayed the third time, saying the same thing.

Then he returned to the disciples and said to them, "Are you still sleeping and resting? Look, the hour is near, and the Son of Man is betrayed into the hands of sinners. Rise, let us go! Here comes my betrayer!"

—Matthew 26:36–46

Betrayers were everywhere. On twelve sides they fled. Judas soon realized the error of his heart, and he took his life. Peter, the big talker, was silent, running for his life. John, the loved one, faltered badly. Thomas, the doubter, was confident of only one thing—that he would run with the rest of the crowd, running from a nightmare into the darkness.

And Jesus was alone.

More likely than not, you'll be there, too, one day. Maybe you've been there already. It happens a lot. Marriage partners disappoint, and then leave. Children watch parents split up, and one leaves. A friendship falters. Depression comes, the joy leaves. Death strikes, and a loved one departs. The result is the same.

Alone.

So maybe you feel empathy for Jesus. Maybe you stand there in the Garden with Jesus and feel the sorrow of being left there—alone.

Or maybe you've run like Andrew, scampered like Thaddaeus, lumbered into the darkness like Matthew. Maybe you and I are just as guilty as Judas of leaving Jesus alone.

Does it surprise you to think about that? It must have surprised the disciples, too, when they were still awake, to hear Jesus say the unthinkable: "You will leave me all alone."

Surely they all denied the very thought. Obviously Jesus' words applied to someone else. *Of all of the people who would leave Jesus alone,* each man must have thought, *surely it won't be me.*

They were surely wrong. Every one of them left, and they didn't waste any time doing it.

How could they live with themselves after such devastating personal failures? Were they gasping for air and holding their chests because of all the running—or were they holding their chests out of horror at what they'd just done?

Somehow these eleven men survived. Somehow they kept putting one foot in front of the other. Somehow they remembered that Jesus loved them despite their failures. Perhaps they concentrated on the other things that Jesus had said in his last few minutes of instruction. For instance, as soon as he dropped the bomb about being left alone, Jesus said something mystical and then mysterious: "Yet I am not alone, for my Father is with me. I have told you these things, so that in me you may have peace. In this world you will have trouble. But take heart! I have overcome the world" (John 16:32b–33).

The Father will be with Jesus. The invisible God would be with a visible man.

And then, those strange words. "Take heart! Be encouraged! Cheer up! There's going to be a lot of trouble, but I've overcome the world." It would be a full weekend before the disciples would begin to understand.

The mass betrayal so dominates the scene in the Garden that it's hard to remember the reasons for the laughter.

Look at the promises. Jesus says that these men will soon be able to ask for anything at all—in his name—and be given it (John 16:23). You could say it this way: they would receive great blessings. Jesus says that as they receive what they ask for, they'll also be given a complete joy (16:24). A moment later (16:27), Jesus says that God the Father loves these scoundrels. Finally, noting his ultimate victory, Jesus promises them peace (16:33).

And Jesus knows, the entire time, that these guys are going to leave him alone as surely as he knows that people today are going to fall far short of perfection. Jesus promised the miraculous to men who would run *toward* temptation about as much as they'd run *from* it. It's a masterpiece of grace, a love that's unbelievable. And it still works today.

And there's one more thing. Because of what happened in the twenty-four hours that followed his last word of teaching, Jesus was able to transfer the peace he had to us. Our peace was provided through the worst day of his life.

Was Jesus alone? His every friend had left. Every support system he knew was taken away. The institutions he should have been able to trust—the government and the religious leaders—weren't trustworthy. His strength was taken away, lash by lash, blow by blow, and nail by nail. His life was stolen, and his body was laid in a cold, stone tomb. He had no brain waves, no heart beat, no blood pressure, and no oxygen.

But through it all, *Jesus wasn't alone.* Do you remember what he had said? *"Yet I am not alone, for my Father is with me."*

And yet, he was alone. Of course, he was alone as he bore the sins of the world. He was alone as he died as the ultimate and final sacrifice. As holy God turned away from the sin that Jesus carried, Jesus was alone. He was alone on purpose, alone with a job to do—alone so that you and I would never have to be alone. There, as he paid the price for our sin, Jesus was alone.

Still, he wasn't alone.

This sounds contradictory, but it's not. It's critically important to realize what happened in the tomb. Jesus didn't raise himself from the dead. God the Father did it for him. Jesus was really dead. Jesus was really helpless, as helpless as any dead human being. Jesus was completely dependent on something to happen on his behalf, something that would have to be done by Another.

Do you see how amazing that is? The Son of God, who had power to keep control, willingly gave up control so he could be like us. You know the truth. When death comes, we'll be utterly without control. We'll step away from this life into a realm of existence that none of us has ever experienced. Once there, we'll be completely dependent upon God to save us. To be precise, we'll die in faith.

By my count, the Bible speaks of the resurrection of Jesus forty-five times. In each of those times, the wording of Scripture makes clear that God the Father took the action of raising Jesus. From the times when Jesus spoke of his resurrection to Peter's preaching on Pentecost to Paul's theological understanding of what happened, it is *always* a case of God the Father raising Jesus, the Son.

In short, Jesus wasn't alone in death. And what's the importance of that? You won't be left alone there, either.

Knowing this assurance leads to a joy that is unlike any other. A peace unlike any other comes from knowing that you'll have security beyond this life and that you won't be left alone. That's why Jesus would end his last six hours of teaching—the most important and passionate teaching that he would give these men—with these words: "I have told you these things, so that in me you may have peace. In this world you will have trouble. But take heart! I have overcome the world" (John 16:33).

Within this passage, Jesus has painted a vivid word picture. Centuries ago, the Greek word that described squeezing an orange for every last drop was *thilpsin*. When a man took a hammer and crushed a date nut, that action was *thilpsin*. Squeezing. Crushing. When Jesus said that these men were going to have trouble, he used the same word. "I want you to have peace, because the day is coming when life will hammer you, squeeze you, and crush you. For you to survive it, I will go through this process myself. In fact, I want you to cheer up, to take courage, to lighten up! Because, you see, I have overcome the world. In every minute of what is about to happen, I will be following the plan so you can have what I've promised you."

Blessings. Joy. Peace.

Can we imagine what has been done on our behalf, so that we can be so richly blessed? Can we comprehend how great a price was paid so that we would never be alone?

Sometimes we can.

A remarkable German family lived in a tiny village near Nuremberg in the fifteenth century. The Dürer household included eighteen children. Eighteen!

Although their father was a goldsmith who worked almost every waking hour providing for his family, the children knew that their chances of achieving their dreams were slim. Two of the older children dreamed of pursuing art as a career, but neither of them nurtured the illusion that their father would be able to send them to the Academy in Nuremberg.

The boys spoke often of their dreams. They confided in each other at night in their crowded bed. Eventually, as they grew older, they made a pact. They would toss a coin. The loser would go down into the nearby mines and, with his earnings, support his brother while he attended the Academy. Then, in four years, when the brother who won the toss completed his studies, he would support the other brother at the Academy, either with sales of his artwork or, if necessary, also by laboring in the mines.

It was on a Sunday when they selected the coin. After church on that sacred day, they tossed the coin. They watched it flip end over end, falling toward a moment that would change their lives.

Albrecht won. Albert lost. Albrecht went to Nuremberg; Albert went into the darkness of the mines. Albrecht studied for free in relative comfort, but Albert labored under inhumane conditions.

Albrecht was an immediate sensation, and his etchings, wood-cuts, and oils were far better than those of most of his professors. By the time he graduated, he was beginning to earn consider-able fees for his commissioned works.

There came a wonderful day after graduation when the Dürer family held a feast on the lawn to celebrate their champion's homecoming. The meal was long, memorable, and attended by many people in the village. Music and laughter provided the back-ground, and Germany's finest new artist sat in honor at the head of the table.

At the end of the meal, Albrecht raised a toast to the one who had paid such an expensive price for his success. His closing words were, "And now, Albert, blessed brother of mine, now it is your turn. Now you can go to Nuremberg to pursue your dream, and I will take care of you."

All heads turned in eager expectation to the far end of the table, where Albert sat. Instead of a man beaming with the prospect of chasing his dream, Albert appeared to be heartbroken. Tears streamed down his pale face. He shook his head, sobbed, and repeated, over and over, "No . . . no . . . no."

Albert rose, wiped away the tears, looked at the faces of his family, and held his hands close to his face. "No, brother. I cannot go to Nuremberg. It is too late for me. Look . . . look what four years in the mines have done to my hands! The bones in every finger have been smashed at least once, and lately I have been suffering from arthritis so badly in my right hand that I cannot even hold a glass to return your toast, much less make delicate lines on parchment or canvas with a pen or a brush. No, brother . . . for me it is too late."

More than four hundred fifty years have passed since that afternoon in a German village when one man realized the price that another man paid for his happiness. By now, Albrecht Dürer's hundreds of masterful portraits, pen and silver-point sketches, watercolors, charcoals, woodcuts, and copper engravings hang in every great museum in the world. Unless you happen to be an art connoisseur, however, you are probably aware of only one of Dürer's works. You might have a reproduction of it in your home or office. Dürer's greatest work of art is the painting of a pair of hands, palms together, thin fingers stretched skyward. The world dubbed them "The Praying Hands," but Albrecht Dürer knew them simply as *Albert's* hands.[1]

Jesus held out his hands to the men who listened to the promises—hands that were about to be destroyed by a Roman hammer, and he said, "Because I love you so much, you will never, ever, ever have to be alone. Not in life, not in death, not in eternity."

Never alone. Albrecht Dürer had the hands of his brother. You've got the hands of Jesus. Take his hands. Love his hands. Cherish his hands. Trust your life to his hands. Once you do, you will never be alone again.

Fourteen

Eavesdropping on a Private Prayer

The amusement park line seemed horribly long. The ticket lady wasn't moving fast, and the children were antsy. A roller coaster train roared through the treetops, almost over our heads. Having the time of their lives, the riders seemed to swoop right down on top of us. They moved at breakneck speed; we didn't move at all.

I looked around at the others waiting in the ticket line. It seemed to be universal. The delighted screams coming from that roller coaster only increased the impatience in our line of the unamused.

Inside the park, just a short distance away, the rides were all coming to life. We could hear them whirring and rolling and buzzing. Some larger-than-life cartoon characters were hugging children and posing for photos. We could see them, just beyond the ticket lady. It was all so frustrating, this waiting for the dream-come-true, this wondering what it would be like to finally grasp that coveted ticket, to finally move toward the cartoon characters, the rides, the food—the fun!

For a child who'd never been to an amusement park—how frustrating to be there, and yet not quite there. To be in line for the tickets while the fun circled and screamed inside was cruel and unusual punishment.

You could take two drastically different photographs that day. One taken in the morning sunlight at the ticket window would show five-year-olds craning their necks, first-graders with big, expectant eyes, little ones straining forward in strollers. But a photograph taken at sunset would show the same children in a completely different, exhausted light. You'd see some being carried on daddies' shoulders, some sleeping soundly in strollers, and some trudging with fatigue toward the exits. None would care that the rides still whirled and rumbled all around them.

The difference? They had *experienced* the amusement park. They had once heard of it, but now they knew it. Sure, they were worn out from the fun, but they were also satisfied and could sleep peacefully.

*   *   *

The auditorium was crowded and stuffy. Designed for two hundred people, the place was packed with nearly four hundred bodies. A college president spoke some words about life, education, and dreams. Another neatly dressed official said something along the same lines.

It's not that the words didn't matter; it's just that they didn't matter much. The parents in the room had been grooming these children for the better part of two decades. A video tape of the event would show children who didn't look like children on the verge of their college years. The kids were well dressed and uncomfortable with all of their parents around. They looked more like adults, and some of them were taller than their parents. The eyes of the graduates revealed a mixture of anticipation, mystery, fear, and anxiety.

They were in the starting blocks at the Kentucky Derby, pushing against the gates. The race was *right in front of them*, and they were ready to run. They were as jittery as green horses, a long way from champions, and their doubts mixed with their confidence, making the entire morning one of the most uncomfortable of their lives.

Record a college video of these same human beings four years later and you'd see young adults who are much more secure with life. They know every inch of the campus and every hour of the daily schedule. They know the traditions of the school. They know the habits of their best friends, people they didn't even know four years before. They also know all of the president's speeches by heart. They're so familiar with college life that they're bored with it. What once thrilled them is now old hat. Some of them had to be pressured to put on a cap and gown.

These once-nervous freshmen have gotten a handle on acquiring knowledge, sorting through it, and using it. They've got a hint of the future, and they're ready to claim it. Now their dreams speak of offices, business contacts, and job interviews. More mature, they strain at this new gate to the future with a little more experience.

What turns an insecure freshman into a mostly secure senior?

Four years makes the difference. Four years of classes, football games, friendships, club meetings, late-night talks, and end-of-semester study sessions. Graduating seniors aren't afraid of class schedules any more because they've finished the course. They're not wondering what food the cafeteria will serve because they've eaten it all (and complained about most of it). The college experience itself is at the core of the knowledge they've gained.

* * *

I've stood with too many grooms to count. They fidget, they pace, they make one more trip to the water fountain. Some of them talk boastfully of their calm nerves and wonder how *she's* doing. They all try to remember where they'll stand, what they'll say, and how they'll hold the crook of the arm. Eventually, there's a musical cue, and we head toward the center of the room.

It's fun to steal a glance at the groom. Watch him the next time you see him. He smiles at his buddies, winks at her friends. He licks his lips and tries to swallow. He shifts from one leg to the other and tries his best to hide his hands.

Watch his eyes. He'll look beyond her mother, sisters, aunts, and uncles. He'll glance at the faces around him, but his gaze will always—*always*—come back to the door where she will arrive.

He beams when she appears, gliding down the church aisle, resting lightly on her father's arm, and as ready to step toward the future as he is. It takes his breath away.

I've learned to expect anything when a bride and a groom arrive front-and-center. When they turn to face me, they've just begun one of the most nerve-wracking experiences of their lives. Facing the preacher, they might do anything. Some laugh, some cry, some appear stoic. They'll smile maturely at one another, they'll make blunders, and they'll search in vain for some moisture in their mouths. Once in a while, one will faint. Sometimes it all happens in the same wedding! But this much is universal: they all wonder what the future holds.

It's no wonder that they take this moment so seriously. He comes to the altar as a single man, and she, too, comes to this place with an air of independence. They each came alone, although they had perhaps dated for years. When they leave, however, they'll leave together. Married. United. Two in one, one from two. What will marriage be like? What will the weight of the commitment feel like? They have more questions than answers, more fears than securities.

In a year or so, you'll see them again. Note how they arrive together and how they leave together. There's a "oneness" about them. They're relaxed, they laugh a lot, and they have a special calmness to their demeanor. They talk of steps taken to turn dreams into reality. The anxiety, the cotton-mouth dryness, and the air of uncertainty are all gone. If they lick their lips these days, it's over dessert.

What made the difference? A year of being married. No more theory but reality. No more wondering. Now, there is knowledge. They have, in a biblical sense, begun to know one another. All they had heard of, they now know.

* * *

We're going to a private place—a quiet place, a place where the world is changing. We're going to eavesdrop on a prayer, slipping up on someone unaware.

Jesus is praying, and John is listening. John, so transformed by the foot-washing that began the evening, has been locked in on every word for six hours or so. Now he is physically exhausted, but he is also beginning to understand as he's never understood before. He's on the threshold of knowing God. Although he must have slept a little at Gethsemane, he was awake long enough to hear Jesus' prayer.

The words are recorded in John 17, and the words have a lot to do with us. Part of the prayer—a very important part—invites us to the same joy of knowing God. This invitation will come *through* John but *from* Jesus.

People instinctively want to know God. They crane their necks, looking in at those who already enjoy the relationship. They nervously look around at the prospects, waiting anxiously on a transforming moment that will send them on their journey. In time—like our children at the park, like college students well into their studies, or like a young married couple—most of those who plunge into Christianity will be completely changed by this satisfying experience. It will be a joy that had never before been imagined.

Early in his prayer, Jesus prays that we'll be able to know both him and the Father. This idea of "knowing" appears dozens of times in the New Testament but never in a more important place.

As we listen in on the prayer, remember where we've been. Some six hours of teaching have preceded this moment. Jesus has washed the feet of the disciples, led them through a Passover meal, instituted the Lord's Supper, and talked to them repeatedly about blessings, joy, and peace. He has offered them love and spoken of their coming failures. He spoke of failure, not to make them feel even worse about their shortcomings, but to tell them that he loves them despite their shortcomings. Only Judas does not receive the words of forgiveness and love. He is completing a plan that will live as the worst betrayal in human history.

Jesus walks with his eleven men under the towering walls of the Temple Mount in Jerusalem, to the quietness of a garden. He is only a few hundred yards from the Eastern Gate, only a short distance away from where, for centuries, lambs had been sacrificed for the sins of people. More lambs would die the next day.

There, in the garden, the Lamb of God prays:

> Father, the time has come. Glorify your Son, that your Son may glorify you. For you granted him authority over all people that he might give eternal life to all those you have given him. *Now this is eternal life: that they may know you, the only true God, and Jesus Christ, whom you have sent.* I have brought you glory on earth by completing the work you

gave me to do. And now, Father, glorify me in your presence
with the glory I had with you before the world began.

—John 17:1–5

Take special note of this incredibly important moment. Jesus
gives a definition of eternal life: "Now this is eternal life: that they
may know you, the only true God, and Jesus Christ, whom you
have sent."

You can know God. You don't have to merely hear about God,
or learn about God, or sing about God. You can know God. You
can be as transformed as a kid leaving the amusement park—
satisfied and at peace. You can be more satisfied than a happy
couple with a year of marriage behind them. You can move
through the experience of knowing Jesus in such a personal way
that you'll have eternal life.

When Jesus prayed in the garden, it must have been around
midnight. When Jesus prayed that we might have eternal life, he
was only nine hours or so from the cross. When Jesus hung on
the cross, the full knowledge of who he was would finally be public. But even there, people would not recognize what God was
doing. Make no mistake, however. It is at the cross where you can
know Jesus at the most essential point in his earthly mission.

Recognizing that mission is not hard. For three years or so, the
miracles had been bearing witness to who Jesus was. His teaching had set him apart as a great rabbi, one sent from God. Supernatural incidents occurred around Jesus that caused the crowds
to wonder if he was the Messiah. His disciples came to believe it.
All of these events had been testifying, whispering, "Jesus is the
Christ. Jesus is the Son of God. Jesus is the way, the truth, the life
. . . follow him."

Then, suddenly, there was the cross. No more whispering. No
more innuendoes. No more hiding in the garden.

At that moment, the cross stood in front of a great rock

outcropping, just outside the city gate, on a main highway. Here, at the crossroads of the world, a man died slowly, and eternity hung in the balance. Even the sign over his head proclaimed the truth: "King of the Jews"! Where once God gave glimpses through the prophets, he turned the spotlight toward an execution with a purpose. Although a few people had already come to believe that Jesus was the Messiah, at that moment God's plan was made fully known by the cross. Yes, it took a weekend before the impact of the Cross was known, but no single event in world history would ever garner such attention.

Even today, people can't deny the impact of the Cross. They may or may not accept the Bible's message about the spiritual importance of the Cross, but no one can ignore it. For centuries, it has changed the entire world. The Cross still speaks most loudly as the way to know God.

Jesus prayed that we might know him, and when he finished his prayer, the road to Skull Hill was set upon.

His prayer was answered with an execution.

Nothing rivals the cross as the center of attention in the Bible. What is amazing, however, is that when Jesus prayed just hours before the cruelty would begin, he prayed little for himself and much for us:

> I have revealed you to those whom you gave me out of the world. They were yours; you gave them to me and they have obeyed your word. Now they know that everything you have given me comes from you. For I gave them the words you gave me and they accepted them. They knew with certainty that I came from you, and they believed that you sent me. I pray for them. I am not praying for the world, but for those you have given me, for they are yours. All I have is yours, and all you have is mine. And glory has come to me through them.
>
> —John 17:6–10

It's amazing that Jesus could look upon that rag-tag group of sleeping scoundrels and talk so fondly of them. They would all betray him within moments, but he spoke of them as if they were the world's greatest men. They had loved Jesus, and Jesus loved them.

Today we, of course, still sleep when we should be alert, and Jesus loves us anyway. In fact, even when the disciples weren't listening, Jesus was praying that you and I would be blessed. When he prayed in the garden, he prayed for good things to happen to you and me.

The blessings of knowing Jesus were the very things about which he prayed there in the Garden of Gethsemane. The blessings aren't hard to spot. He prays first of all that we would have unity with other believers: "I will remain in the world no longer, but they are still in the world, and I am coming to you. Holy Father, protect them by the power of your name—the name you gave me—*so that they may be one as we are one*" (John 17:11).

This unity is obviously important. Twice in this prayer alone, he prays that his followers will be unified. Unity will be one of our weapons, a unity of peace and joy in the midst of a troubled world.

Second, Jesus prays that we would know the full measure of his joy. He has promised his followers for three years, and for the past six hours, that they could have joy. Full and abundant joy. In his prayer for us, he asks the Father to allow us to have that joy: "I am coming to you now, but I say these things while I am still in the world, so that they may have the full measure of my joy within them" (John 17:13).

Think of a sponge that's been soaking in water for a while. As you pick it up, the sponge can't contain all the liquid. It drips water from every pore, even as it holds much more water inside. It has, you might say, a "full measure" of water.

That's the word picture that Jesus wants you to grasp. He didn't ask that we simply be somewhat happy with life; Jesus asked the Father to give us the heavyweight measure of joy. He asked that we have so much joy in our lives that we drip it all over the people we touch.

As we eavesdrop on this prayer, Jesus also prays for something unusual. He prays that we would know the joy of the battle. That's right. Jesus prayed that we'd enjoy the battle. Headed for his toughest battle, Jesus prays that we'll have all that we need for our toughest days.

> I have given them your word and the world has hated them, for they are not of the world any more than I am of the world. My prayer is not that you take them out of the world but that you protect them from the evil one. They are not of the world, even as I am not of it. Sanctify them by the truth; your word is truth. As you sent me into the world, I have sent them into the world. For them I sanctify myself, that they too may be truly sanctified.
>
> —John 17:14–19

Jesus already knows that the world will hate those who believe in him as the Christ. Instead of praying that we'd never have to do battle, however, he prays for our protection in the midst of the battle. Although Satan will try to harm us, Jesus prayed that we would come through the attacks alive and stronger because of the battle.

Our common prayer is, of course, that we could avoid the battle altogether. We don't like the unpleasant. We don't want the struggle. But on the last night of his life before the cross, Jesus prayed primarily that we'd be *in* the battle.

Why shouldn't there be a battle? We are in the world, but not of the world. We wear a different uniform and provide targets for the enemy. But we have different—and incredibly effective—

weapons. We are set apart, or sanctified. We're completely different and are meant to be that way. The purpose for this setting aside? To fight!

If you've not known the joy of the battle, get to know it. If you've not seen people transformed by the truth of Christ, see it. Make it happen. Get off the sidelines, get out of the church pews, and get into the battle. Be in the Word of God, be immersed in the truth, soak up the joy, and then watch the battle lines fall into place. The peace that you have will be a great weapon. So will your joy. The blessings that fall on you will befuddle those who don't understand Christians who experience the abundant life. You will make a difference in things spiritual.

Time is running short at this point in Jesus' prayer. Judas is leading an army of soldiers prepared for battle toward the very place where the disciples sleep and the Savior prays.

There is time for one more truth, one more life-changing insight. As Jesus prayed, he made sure that he prayed for people living centuries after that midnight in the garden: "My prayer is not for them alone. I pray also for *those who will believe in me through their message . . ."* (John 17:20).

Isn't that incredible? Jesus looked through the pages of history, saw you, and prayed for you!

> That all of them may be one, Father, just as you are in me and I am in you. May they also be in us so that the world may believe that you have sent me. I have given them the glory that you gave me, that they may be one as we are one: I in them and you in me. May they be brought to complete unity to let the world know that you sent me and have loved them even as you have loved me.
>
> —John 17:21–23

It's worth noting that when he prayed for those of us in the twenty-first-century church, he prayed again for our unity. Then, he simply breaks down into a love song:

> Father, I want those you have given me to be with me where I am, and to see my glory, the glory you have given me because you loved me before the creation of the world.
>
> Righteous Father, though the world does not know you, I know you, and they know that you have sent me. I have made you known to them, and will continue to make you known in order that the love you have for me may be in them and that I myself may be in them.
>
> —John 17:24–26

Do you see the simple truth here? Jesus says, "Father, I want these to be with me, with us." Did the angels scratch their heads, looking at the snoring cowards in the garden? Did they wonder if Jesus could see how far short of God's glory we'd fall? Were they amazed that the Father didn't object, that he, indeed, wanted us to be with him?

No, Jesus said it simply: "I want those you have given me to be with me where I am." I want them to see the glory of heaven, the glory of eternity. I am willing to go to the cross to get them there. That's how much I love them.

And then, in his very last words of the prayer, Jesus asks that we would have his presence with us while we lived on the earth. He prays, asking that "I myself may be in them."

Amazing. He looks at men who don't deserve it and asks permission to bring them into laughter. He sees, so to speak, the faces of kids at an amusement park—kids who really want to get inside. "Father," Jesus prays, "can they have the full measure of my joy?" Jesus sees the faces of nervous students, just starting a journey that scares them. "Father," Jesus prays, "I pray that they'd really know us. Not just head knowledge, but the knowledge of experience." And Jesus looks at our hearts that are as jittery as a bride and a groom awaiting the ceremony, and prays for our peace. "Father," he prays, "I eventually want them to be where I am, and right now, I want my presence to be with them."

*   *   *

Reading these words about attaining blessings, joy, and peace, I realize that a lot of it sounds like theory—far removed from reality. I hate to say it, but it sounds like a sermon.

I asked myself the question that many people ask themselves as they read the prayer of Jesus in the garden. Can people really have joy in life, especially in the midst of difficult times?

Then I remembered the day that John dropped by my office. He had just been unjustly fired, and the prospects for finding a similar job were almost zero. His wife was anxious, to say the least, and my emotions ranged between grief and rage. John, however, was upbeat. He was so excited about the opportunity to pursue his dreams that he ignored my anxiety. He was certain that God was going to provide a job with better working conditions, and he was convinced that much of the reason for his firing was so he could have more family time in the evenings. But mainly, he was convinced that God was at work in his life. The smile on his face was genuine, and the laughter from his heart was infectious.

In a few weeks, John was at work in a new job, one that would become satisfying, professionally and personally.

And I remember Joe. His battle with cancer had already taken up the better part of a decade, and he'd just received news that he would experience one more round of treatments, surgeries, and pain. The difference this time, the doctor had told him, was that the pain would only prolong his life, not save it.

Joe had stopped by my office to catch his breath emotionally before he shared the news with his wife. And as we talked, Joe noticed that my emotions were dropping lower and lower as the reality of his words hit home.

"Wait a minute," Joe said. "You need to know something. Cancer is the best thing that has ever happened to me."

I suppose that my face registered my astonishment.

"You see," he continued, "I didn't pay attention to the Lord until I got cancer. I was never serious about my walk with the Lord until I went through all of this. The last few years of my life have been the best because I've been closer to him than ever. I'm telling you, cancer has been the best thing that ever happened to me."

And with those simple words, he leaned back, took a few more relaxing breaths, and prepared to head toward his future.

The cancer took his life a few months later, but nothing took away his joy.

I think, too, of the other families and individuals who've taught me about joy, about peace, about blessings in the midst of battle. I don't think any of them pulled out a book like this one, or tried to analyze the prayer of John 17 line by line. No, they simply possessed the joy. Jesus had prayed for them, and the prayer of the Son of God had been answered powerfully and literally.

All of these people sought a relationship with Jesus first, then invested years of serious discipleship, and then reaped enormous benefits of joy when they needed those benefits most.

If you're in need of joy today, I invite you to go back to Gethsemane, slip in beside John, and listen to Jesus pray for you.

Fifteen

The Laughter of a Champion

It may have been cloudy or clear, sunny or hazy. We get no hints of the day being anything but normal when on Mount Horeb, the mountain of God, Moses spied a bush that was on fire. Certainly, it got his attention. It was a fiery aberration in the middle of nowhere, a curiosity that demanded his focus.

But this burning bush wasn't destroying the leaves. The branches were brown, not black. The smoke was eerie, and the flames were supernatural.

I suppose that the whole world knows the story of how God spoke to Moses from the midst of the bush, of how Moses threw off his sandals and fell face down in the presence of God. There, on that ground, suddenly holy, Moses heard God's command to rescue the Hebrew slaves, and there in front of that frightening bush, Moses tried to sidestep a terrifying job assignment. In Jewish perspective, the apex of the conversation came early on, when Moses pulled a stunt that should have cost him his life.

He asked God for his name.

Moses said to God, "Suppose I go to the Israelites and say to them, 'The God of your fathers has sent me to you,' and they ask me, 'What is his name?' Then what shall I tell them?"

God said to Moses, "I AM WHO I AM. This is what you are to say to the Israelites: 'I AM has sent me to you.'"

—Exodus 3:13–14

Scholars have wrestled to this very moment with what that phrase means, exactly. "I AM WHO I AM" is a strange name, you'd agree, and it points to the difficulty of putting into human letters God's self-identification. Look at how modern translators try to say it:

I AM THAT I AM.

—KING JAMES VERSION

I AM WHAT I AM.

—THE BIBLE IN BASIC ENGLISH[1]

I AM; that is who I am.

—NEW ENGLISH BIBLE[2]

I AM BECAUSE I AM.

—SPURRELL[3]

I am the God who is.

—KNOX[4]

I-will-be-what-I-will-be.

—JAMES MOFFATT TRANSLATION[5]

I Will Become whatsoever I please.

—THE EMPHASIZED BIBLE[6]

I Am He who is.

—NEW JERUSALEM BIBLE[7]

Can you imagine the mental wrestling in scholars' libraries? Can you hear the debate over those mysterious Hebrew letters? It's been going on for centuries.

The debate became even more important about 250 years before Jesus was born in Bethlehem. The Jewish people had become scattered, and an entire generation was growing up with no knowledge of the Hebrew Bible. Greek was the language of most of the world, and the God-fearing people in Israel wanted their people to know their Scriptures. Therefore, a translation of the Hebrew Bible into Greek was ordered. Ancient reports say that it was completed in Alexandria, in the middle of the third century B.C., by seventy Hebrew scholars. They wrestled with every book, every chapter and, in cases such as Exodus 3, every word.

Could there have been a more important moment than when the scholars determined what to write as an accurate representation of God's name? The burning bush created a burning debate. Eventually, there came a simple phrase in Greek letters that would go down in this Septuagint, this new, ground-breaking translation of the Hebrew Bible.

The words they chose? *Ego-eimi.*

From that day forth, the common phrase *Ego-eimi* would have a sacred meaning, especially when it was used in a sacred context. It would be so sacred that it would hardly be spoken. But it was spoken on the last night of Jesus' earthly life.

There in Gethsemane, beneath the olive trees, Jesus was confronted by the mob. The disciples awoke and felt their hearts in their throats. Judas arrived, delivered the worst kiss of all history, and handed Jesus over to an army. The eleven disciples ran as fast as their legs would carry them into the darkness.

John's gospel is specific about the soldiers who arrived in the

garden that night. It was a "cohort," or a "band," of Roman soldiers. At full strength, a cohort was six hundred soldiers, at par-
tial strength a minimum of two hundred. Years later, the apostle
Paul would be escorted to Caesarea by a similar cohort of 200
soldiers, plus at least 270 more armed guards (see Acts 23:23).

The cohort that came to arrest Jesus looked nothing like those
depicted in modern Easter pageants—three Roman soldiers
thumping down the church aisle. *Hundreds* of soldiers were at
Gethsemane. This scene was real life with real Romans who pre-
ferred to overwhelm all opponents.

The soldiers had been told that twelve men were in the valley,
some of them armed and one with miraculous powers. Those
twelve men had often rallied crowds of thousands of people, so a
battle was a distinct possibility. The best bet, they knew, was to
slip up on the twelve men while they were isolated, take their
leader, and retreat quickly inside the Roman headquarters.

The plan was going wonderfully well.

Judas led them to Jesus, and no violence seemed to be
forthcoming. Oh, there was that laughable moment when Simon
Peter cut off the ear of a servant, but that was the only bloodshed.
In the confusion, most of the soldiers must have noticed that the
ear didn't even seem to be damaged. There had been a brief
contact by the miracle worker, and the fighting, the bloodshed,
and the ear attacks were all over.

John tells the story:

> When he had finished praying, Jesus left with his disciples
> and crossed the Kidron Valley. On the other side there was
> an olive grove, and he and his disciples went into it.
>
> Now Judas, who betrayed him, knew the place, because
> Jesus had often met there with his disciples. So Judas came
> to the grove, guiding a detachment of soldiers and some of-
> ficials from the chief priests and Pharisees. They were car-
> rying torches, lanterns and weapons.

Jesus, knowing all that was going to happen to him, went out and asked them, "Who is it you want?"

"Jesus of Nazareth," they replied.

"I am he," Jesus said. (And Judas the traitor was standing there with them.) When Jesus said, "I am he," *they drew back and fell to the ground.*

—John 18:1–6

Note what was said in the Greek language. They didn't speak English, of course, but Greek, the language that Alexander the Great had given to the world. They spoke, you might say, in the language of the Septuagint.

"Who is it you want?" Jesus asked.

"Jesus of Nazareth," they replied.

Jesus' reply? *"Ego-eimi."*

And with those words, two hundred or more soldiers, dozens of religious leaders, a handful of temple guards, political body guards, and Judas the betrayer fell back as if a sudden wind had rushed through the olive trees. The soldiers fell back in embarrassment, the religious leaders fell back in indignation, and Judas fell back with the shock of the unexpected.

The soldiers had trained at their version of Parris Island. They were the strongest men in Jerusalem and were armed to the teeth. They were used to violence, and they had already been tested in war. But in the span of four syllables, they stumbled. They faltered. They met something more powerful than they had expected. As one translation (WILLIAMS)[8] puts it, they "took a lurch backward."

The moment marked the beginning of the most familiar part of Jesus' life—his crucifixion and resurrection. But right then it was midnight in the garden. By noon the next day, Jesus would be so cruelly beaten, so badly scourged, and so horribly disfigured that it would have been difficult for even his friends to recognize him. In many people's eyes, he was and is the biggest loser of history, the worst-beaten man ever to walk the roads of hoped-for stardom, the most defeated pretender to importance.

But the Bible presents Jesus in quite a different light. He was, without doubt, who he claimed to be, the same power who once spoke from a burning bush on the back side of a deserted mountain. He was with God, and he *was* God. He was God in human flesh, different from the Father, different from the Spirit, but at the same time exactly the same!

His time on the cross would prove that Jesus really was who he said he was.

> "I and the Father are one."
>
> —John 10:30

> "Anyone who has seen me has seen the Father."
>
> —John 14:9

> "Holy Father, protect them by the power of your name—the name you gave me—so that they may be one as we are one."
>
> —John 17:11

> *"Ego-eimi."*
>
> —John 18:5

Add the following title to the list of who Jesus was: Champion. Never forget where Jesus is now. He is at the right hand of the Father, crowned with all glory and surrounded by more praise and honor than can be described by human words.

Looking closely at the events of those excruciating hours after Gethsemane, you'll see that Jesus was clearly in command of what appeared to be totally out of control.

But before we take that look, perhaps you'd like to know *why* we're taking a closer look at the cross. What difference does it make if Jesus handled his crucifixion better than the thousands who had already been nailed to Roman crosses? What difference would it make to call him the Champion on the cross?

Because you're on his team. Or at least you *can* be on his team.

I've been around great athletes long enough to know—you hang around with champions, and you become one. Teams hire championship coaches, men and women who've taken their teams to the top, and sure enough, the team starts playing better, winning more, climbing toward the championship level. When a team brings in a proven winner—a crack quarterback, a Cy Young Award-winning pitcher, or last year's MVP basketball player—it simply expects to win.

If you watch Jesus on the worst day of his life, it will help you in the worst days of your life. Watch the Champion.

Just as a champion would do it, Jesus walked willingly toward the battle, willingly toward the last hours of his life.

Look at the evidence: "Jesus, *knowing all that was going to happen to him,* went out and asked them, 'Who is it you want?'" (John 18:4).

John, the gospel writer, didn't have to guess what Jesus was thinking about or make up his own opinion. For several days after the Resurrection, John had a chance to talk with Jesus on the championship side of the cross. Surely John gained much of his insight on the life of Christ not only from being an eyewitness to the events but also from what Jesus said to him after the terror was over.

And Jesus *"went out and asked them."* Jesus didn't wait for the mob to come to him. He went to them. He was on the offensive, and he was the aggressor. He was, in short, acting like a champion. He had no fear of his opponent.

Like a champion, Jesus remained in control when he faced confrontation with the three most powerful, most feared men in Jerusalem. Caiaphas, the corrupt high priest and the most important Jewish man in Israel, had the influence to have a man killed. Pilate had friends in high places and a signature powerful enough to get a man executed. And Herod had the title and the genealogy as well as the reputation of being a brutal king. Watch the encounters that Jesus had with all three men. Despite the fearful—even brutal—environment in each setting, Jesus was controlling the events.

In front of Caiaphas, Jesus was largely silent. The charges against Jesus were false and horribly out of context. The trial was illegal and the setting unfair.

> Then the high priest stood up and said to Jesus, "Are you not going to answer? What is this testimony that these men are bringing against you?"
>
> But Jesus remained silent.
>
> The high priest said to him, "I charge you under oath by the living God: Tell us if you are the Christ, the Son of God."
>
> "Yes, it is as you say," Jesus replied. "But I say to all of you: In the future you will see the Son of Man sitting at the right hand of the Mighty One and coming on the clouds of heaven."
>
> Then the high priest tore his clothes and said, "He has spoken blasphemy! Why do we need any more witnesses? Look, now you have heard the blasphemy. What do you think?"
>
> "He is worthy of death," they answered.
>
> Then they spit in his face and struck him with their fists. Others slapped him and said, "Prophesy to us, Christ. Who hit you?"
>
> —Matthew 26:62–68

Looking at this exchange, remember, Caiaphas *knew* that the testimony against Jesus was false. Jesus also knew that it was false, but he chose to remain silent. When words were needed, Jesus didn't hesitate, he didn't stutter, and he stunned the man who had the position of control. Caiaphas resorted to the ultimate reaction of anger, tearing the most sacred suit of clothes in all of Israel. Yes, it was a difficult setting, a fearful and painful confrontation, but Jesus remained in control.

In front of Herod, with a noisy group of accusers shouting in the room, Jesus elected not to say one word.

> When Herod saw Jesus, he was greatly pleased, because for a long time he had been wanting to see him. From what he had heard about him, he hoped to see him perform some miracle. He plied him with many questions, *but Jesus gave him no answer.* The chief priests and the teachers of the law were standing there, vehemently accusing him.
>
> —Luke 23:8–10

Against Pilate, Jesus faced his most critical moment. Pilate was the man who could send him to the cross. He was also the man who could save his neck, and you can almost sense that Pilate wanted to help Jesus. He talked about the ministry of Jesus, he philosophized about "truth," he heard a warning from his wife, and finally he washed his hands of the matter. One gets the feeling that if Jesus had simply shouted for justice or appealed for mercy, there would have been no cross.

> As soon as the chief priests and their officials saw him, they shouted, "Crucify! Crucify!"
>
> But Pilate answered, "You take him and crucify him. As for me, I find no basis for a charge against him."
>
> The Jews insisted, "We have a law, and according to that law he must die, because he claimed to be the Son of God."
>
> When Pilate heard this, he was even more afraid, and he

went back inside the palace. "Where do you come from?" he asked Jesus, but Jesus gave him no answer. "Do you refuse to speak to me?" Pilate said. "Don't you realize I have power either to free you or to crucify you?"

Jesus answered, "You would have no power over me if it were not given to you from above. Therefore the one who handed me over to you is guilty of a greater sin."

From then on, Pilate tried to set Jesus free, but the Jews kept shouting, "If you let this man go, you are no friend of Caesar. Anyone who claims to be a king opposes Caesar."

When Pilate heard this, he brought Jesus out and sat down on the judge's seat at a place known as the Stone Pavement (which in Aramaic is Gabbatha). It was the day of Preparation of Passover Week, about the sixth hour.

"Here is your king," Pilate said to the Jews.

But they shouted, "Take him away! Take him away! Crucify him!"

"Shall I crucify your king?" Pilate asked.

"We have no king but Caesar," the chief priests answered.

Finally Pilate handed him over to them to be crucified.

—John 19:6–16

Again, in a pressure-packed atmosphere, Jesus spoke only when he wanted to speak, and he said only what he wanted to say. His words were bold, sure, and without a crack in the voice. Jesus was in control of his emotions, his answers, and his actions. The three leaders, however, the three men with titles of power, had no control. The real power lay in the hands of Jesus. He knew what was going to happen to him, walked willingly toward it, and remained solidly in control in a situation that appeared out of control.

Finally, like a champion, Jesus excelled in his most difficult hour. Simply put, he was the Champion on the cross. Unlike the other two men beside him on crosses, Jesus didn't curse his torturers. Perhaps he was the first man in history not to do so. Surely, he was the first crucified man to pray for the men who put him on a cross (Luke 23:34).

On the cross, Jesus took care of his mother's needs, asking John, the disciple, to care for her.

Jesus remained aware of his task, and he refused even the mildest drug that would have numbed his senses and dulled his pain (see Matt. 27:34).

Jesus quoted Scripture and pointed all who heard him to the plan of salvation.

> And at the ninth hour Jesus cried out in a loud voice, *"Eloi, Eloi, lama sabachthani?"*—which means, "My God, my God, why have you forsaken me?"
>
> —Mark 15:33

Are you wondering about the passage that Jesus quoted? It was Psalm 22, easily the most evangelistic of the psalms, and one that is most closely associated with the cross. That ancient song begins with the haunting words, "My God, my God, why have you forsaken me?" Jesus wanted people at the foot of the cross to know that this "defeat" was actually God's plan—and the victory.

Finally, Jesus timed his death with the evening, or 3:00 P.M., sacrifice. As a lamb died for sin *inside* the city, the Lamb of God died for the sin of the world *outside* the city, saying as he died, "It is finished."

All of this took place by means of the most horrible form of execution ever created. Jesus completed his task on the cross despite the greatest emotional, physical, and spiritual pain of his life. Only a champion—the Champion of champions—could have pulled it off.

Again, what does this mean for us? What can we gain by being associated with the Champion?

First, Satan is defeated. If there's a champion, there must be a loser. And Satan lost. On the cross, Christ forever defeated Satan's hold on people.

I heard the story of a missionary who returned to his home in Africa only to find a huge python inside. He ran back to his truck and got his .45 caliber pistol. He returned and warily entered the home through the door. The man aimed with precision and fired a single shot into the snake's head. It was a mortal blow, but the snake didn't die instantly. Instead, as the missionary retreated from his house, the snake thrashed violently.

The tremendous power of the snake's movement broke and damaged many items within the home. After the house finally became silent, the missionary slowly reentered and found a disaster. The snake had broken furniture and accessories, and generally had made a mess of things. But because the snake was dead and had finally run out of life, there was peace.

Satan received, so to speak, a fatal shot to his head when Christ conquered sin and death. At the moment, he seems to be writhing in the pain of his defeat and even unleashing a few remaining, dying, destructive blows. But never forget that, because of the Champion on the cross, although Satan might still be dangerous, his fate is sealed. He might have even torn your life to shreds, but he's not the champion. Stay with Jesus.

Second, you can live like a champion, too. Jesus didn't die so that we could lock him inside churches and theology books. Jesus died so that we could live like champions right now. The Cross set us free. It set us free from the bondage of sin and from the power of fear. If Jesus could look fear in the face and overcome it, so can we.

Remember the words of Paul? He knew the difference that the Cross had made in his life: "For the message of the cross is foolishness to those who are perishing, but to us who are being saved it is the power of God" (1 Cor. 1:18).

As for the victory of the Champion, Paul saw that, too: "Having disarmed the powers and authorities, [Jesus] made a public spectacle of them, triumphing over them by the cross" (Col. 2:15).

Satan thought that he had made a public display of Jesus as a trophy but, in reality, the tables had been turned. It was Satan who had been made the "public spectacle."

Paul saw his life completely transformed by the Cross, and so can you. You can even help add to the "public spectacle" that is being made of Satan. Every time you turn away from temptation by the power of the Cross, you're living like a champion!

Finally, because of the Champion on the cross, we know that we will live forever with him.

The lessons we get from Jesus at this point are lessons of observation. The teachings of the Upper Room and the prayer in the garden are far removed from the public execution in front of Skull Hill. As we look upon the cross, we would be wise to remember *why* all of this happened. Jesus told us why. He looked into the eyes of men who had no idea that he would really die for them in a matter of hours, and said,

> Do not let your hearts be troubled. Trust in God; trust also in me. In my Father's house are many rooms; if it were not so, I would have told you. I am going there to prepare a place for you. And if I go and prepare a place for you, I will come back and take you to be with me that you also may be where I am. . . . I have told you now before it happens, so that when it does happen, you will believe.
>
> —John 14:1–3, 29

Do you believe? Jesus is the Champion of champions, and to be a winner all you have to do is join his team. It's a wonderful invitation. Will you accept? Have you accepted?

In a world of questions, are you looking for *the* Answer? Listen for it.

"Ego-eimi."

Sixteen

The Joy of the Secret

There's nothing quite like it.

The joy of turning off the lights on Christmas Eve, knowing that your work is going to bring squeals of joy to your children at daylight.

The joy of a young wife when she alone knows the results of the pregnancy test. And that moment of private delight is intensified by the anticipation of the joy that news of a coming baby will bring.

The delight that a doctor has just before he calls a patient with good news on test results.

It's the joy of a secret.

We know the story well—about the cross, the tomb, the rolled-away stone, the angels, and the way the news shook Jerusalem. Resurrection morning brought the news of Jesus, the crucified, appearing again, very much alive. We've heard the story as told through the eyes of Mary, Peter, and John. We've doubted with

Thomas and shouted with delight with the two men on the road to Emmaus. Is there any angle that we've forgotten to cover?

Maybe one. What was it like on resurrection morning to be Jesus?

We know from the accounts of that miraculous morning that Jesus was in the garden. We know from John's record of events that Jesus had planned first to return to the Father and then to present himself to the disciples. We know this from his words to Mary, who had fallen at his feet: Jesus said, "Do not hold on to me, for I have not yet returned to the Father. Go instead to my brothers and tell them, 'I am returning to my Father and your Father, to my God and your God'" (John 20:17).

But before that would happen, Jesus was overcome with the joy of the secret. He just couldn't keep it to himself. Learning what happened is worth our time.

Hide in the garden with Jesus, and watch the events unfold. First, according to Matthew, Mark, and Luke, as the earliest hints of sunlight lit the path, Mary Magdalene, Mary the mother of James, Salome, and a woman named Joanna came to the tomb. They were numb with grief, sleepwalking after a weekend of mourning.

Did Jesus see them stop suddenly, stunned by the open tomb, or by the motionless Roman soldiers? Did he listen as the angels announced the news of his resurrection? If he saw and heard it all, did that familiar smile cross his face?

The women ran back quickly and, before long, John and Peter arrived at the tomb. They were gasping for breath after their run through the city streets. If they had investigated the garden as thoroughly as they investigated the tomb, perhaps they would have been the first to see Jesus.

So Peter and the other disciple started for the tomb. Both were running, but the other disciple outran Peter and reached the tomb first. He bent over and looked in at the strips of linen lying there but did not go in. Then Simon Peter, who was behind him, arrived and went into the tomb. He saw the strips of linen lying there, as well as the burial cloth that had been around Jesus' head. The cloth was folded up by itself, separate from the linen. Finally the other disciple, who had reached the tomb first, also went inside. He saw and believed. (They still did not understand from Scripture that Jesus had to rise from the dead.)

Then the disciples went back to their homes. . . .

—John 20:3–10

Somewhere in the garden, Jesus still held his secret, and he was determined to carry on with the plan. He would return to the Father and later appear to these beloved followers. The secret would wait for later in the day.

But something happened that caused the Son of God to change his plan. Something happened that was so traumatic that he couldn't leave without sharing the joy of the secret.

Mary returned.

Then the disciples went back to their homes, but Mary stood outside the tomb crying. As she wept, she bent over to look into the tomb and saw two angels in white, seated where Jesus' body had been, one at the head and the other at the foot.

They asked her, "Woman, why are you crying?"

"They have taken my Lord away," she said, "and I don't know where they have put him."

—John 20:10–13

There is truth here that could transform your life. According to a plan set in motion before the first moments of creation, the Son of God would die for the sin of the world, be resurrected to life by the Father, and then return to the Father. The fulfillment of that plan was to be a celestial, heavenly accomplishment that had been thousands of human years in the making and was in the heart of God from before the beginning. There would be a glorious, thunderous, heavenly welcome, complete with angels, heavenly beings, and all of the faithful who had died, somehow knowing that this day would come. The complete plan is far beyond our understanding, but it was so arranged that Jesus would allow at least six of his followers to come to the tomb, suffer the confusion of the empty tomb, and leave without sharing the joy of the secret. Jesus remained hidden in the garden, preparing for his meeting with the Father.

Suddenly, the plan changed.

Why? The plan changed when Jesus saw one of his followers hurting. She didn't just investigate the tomb, she wept there. She wasn't simply trying to restore some order to the confusion, she was trying to live through a broken heart. She had come to the garden with only a little life, and now it seemed that even that life was gone.

Jesus couldn't bear the sight or the sound of it. He put all of heaven on hold so he could spend just a moment with Mary. He *would not* leave her hopeless. He would not leave her without a reason for joy, a reason for living.

And Jesus won't leave you hopeless, either. He clearly stated that he wanted you to know "complete joy," peace, and blessings. To give those things to you, Jesus will put heaven on hold again, if necessary.

As Mary wept, Jesus took his wonderful detour and stepped out of hiding. She was weeping to the point of not even being able to speak clearly, unable even to distinguish the angels at the tomb or their message.

At this, she turned around and saw Jesus standing there, but she did not realize that it was Jesus.

"Woman," he said, "why are you crying? Who is it you are looking for?"

Thinking he was the gardener, she said, "Sir, if you have carried him away, tell me where you have put him, and I will get him."

Jesus said to her, "Mary."

—John 20:14–16a

Practice saying Mary's name a few times. Did Jesus say it with a whisper? "Mary."

Did he shout it? "MARY!"

Did his eyes light up and twinkle with the greatest secret ever to be revealed? Was it spoken the way one friend would greet another in a long-awaited airport reunion? *"MARY!"*

However it was said, there's no doubt about one thing: Mary instantly realized *who* had called her name. Mary realized that what she could not have hoped for was true. Jesus was alive!

She turned toward him and cried out in Aramaic, "Rabboni!" (which means Teacher).

Jesus said, "Do not hold on to me, for I have not yet returned to the Father. Go instead to my brothers and tell them, 'I am returning to my Father and your Father, to my God and your God.'"

Mary Magdalene went to the disciples with the news: "I have seen the Lord!" And she told them that he had said these things to her.

—John 20:16b–18

After his eventual meeting with the Father, other Resurrection Sunday appearances were made, more people with whom to share the secret.

There was the encounter on the road to Emmaus, when two men suddenly realized that the stranger walking with them was none other than Jesus.

> When he was at the table with them, he took bread, gave thanks, broke it and began to give it to them. Then their eyes were opened and they recognized him, and he disappeared from their sight. They asked each other, "Were not our hearts burning within us while he talked with us on the road and opened the Scriptures to us?"
>
> They got up and returned at once to Jerusalem. There they found the Eleven and those with them, assembled together and saying, "It is true! The Lord has risen and has appeared to Simon."
>
> —Luke 24:30–34

In moments, they had been transformed by the secret.

Note, too, that the above passage gives insight to another private resurrection appearance. "The Lord has risen and has appeared to Simon."

What must that have been like? The one who denied him was meeting the One who forgives! Can we begin to comprehend the joy that Peter must have felt? We can, if we have comprehended our own forgiveness.

Then came the first of several meetings Jesus held with the group.

> On the evening of that first day of the week, when the disciples were together, with the doors locked for fear of the Jews, Jesus came and stood among them and said, "Peace be with you!" After he said this, he showed them his hands and side. The disciples were overjoyed when they saw the Lord.

Again Jesus said, "Peace be with you! As the Father has sent me, I am sending you." And with that he breathed on them and said, "Receive the Holy Spirit. If you forgive anyone his sins, they are forgiven; if you do not forgive them, they are not forgiven."

—John 20:19–23

Here can be drawn two, final, life-changing truths. If you grasp these truths, and these alone, from all I've said, you'll have laughter to last a lifetime. You'll have joy that overflows and peace that transforms every situation, no matter how difficult or mundane the circumstances.

Blessings, peace, and joy. Would you like to claim them?

Here's the first truth: *The difference between fear and joy is the presence of Jesus.*

Consider this picture. Ten men in a dark room, hiding from Roman soldiers, Jewish leaders, angry crowds, and past failures. They might well be anyone, hiding from failed marriages, broken relationships, or miserable track records. They might well have been hiding from whatever makes up the worst chapter of *your* life.

Their doors were "locked for *fear,*" as John phrased it. He knew—he was there.

But in the midst of this fear-charged, failure-bathed environment, Jesus appeared. The Bible says, "Jesus came and stood among them." Jesus stood in their midst, that is, in the middle of them. He didn't stand behind a pulpit and lecture, he didn't stand behind a judge's bench and scold. He stood in their midst and touched them. He blessed them. He showed them his wounds, not waiting for them to voice their doubts. He shared the secret personally, and his smile was reflected in the face of every man.

The laughter in that room must have sounded like a shout. The surprise must have sounded like a child's squeals of delight when he bounds into the living room on Christmas morning. Their shouts must have been like the shouts of a daddy-to-be when he first hears the news from his wife: "We're expecting!" The disciples' relief must have been the relief that a patient feels when the physician relays good news instead of bad. On second thought, all of those emotions must have been multiplied a hundred times over.

Jesus was in the room. He had been dead, but now he was alive. They had been witnesses to tragedy, but now they touched a miracle. They had been afraid, but now they had joy. In fact, John says that they were "overjoyed." They couldn't contain it. They were thrilled and delighted, nearly insane with the presence of Christ.

And that, my friend, is the core truth of what I'm communicating. The only difference between fear and joy in that room two thousand years ago was the presence of Jesus. When Jesus was there, fear was immediately changed into joy. The change was instantaneous and undeniable. It was unstoppable. And the moment was life changing.

The same kind of change happens today when Jesus makes an appearance in a life. I've seen it in the eyes of a woman, relieved that she finally gave her life to Christ. I've heard it in the voice of a man, joyful because he's given his heart to Jesus. I've watched it in the joy of teenagers, ecstatic that they've been forgiven and empowered by the Spirit of Christ. I've seen it in my own life.

There is no substitute, no alternative way to life, no other way to find the joy, the blessings, or the peace that Jesus has to offer. Only the presence of Jesus in your life can make this possible.

How can that be possible today, when Jesus doesn't make regular appearances behind the locked doors of our homes? It's simple. Even without seeing the events, we can read of the Cross and of the Resurrection and hear of the miracles and the teaching and the life of Jesus, and believe that his life was given as a ransom for our own. We can give our lives completely to him, yielding our will to his will, our decisions to his standard. The moment we make that commitment, the day we decide to walk with him, Jesus comes into our hearts as surely as he came into that locked room of fearful disciples.

Do you remember what Jesus said when he took away Thomas's doubts? These words are about you. Jesus told him, "Because you have seen me, you have believed; blessed are those who have not seen and yet have believed" (John 20:29).

Even John was concerned about you. As he ended his writing of the life, death, and resurrection of Jesus, he was aware that many more generations would be reading these words, and considering the choice of a lifetime. Look at his words:

> Jesus did many other miraculous signs in the presence of his disciples, which are not recorded in this book. But these are written *that you may believe that Jesus is the Christ, the Son of God, and that by believing you may have life in his name.*
>
> —John 20:30–31

So there's a central truth to the abundant life: the difference between fear and joy is the presence of Jesus in your life.

Here's a final principle drawn from this passage: *Joy leads to ministry.*

When you find the joy that Jesus promised, you won't be able to stop the ministry that comes naturally from your life. You wouldn't want to stop it if you could.

In the wake of his appearance, while the joy was still new, Jesus revealed a new role for the disciples to play. Go back to those first few seconds of shouting and overwhelming joy.

On the evening of that first day of the week, when the

disciples were together, with the doors locked for fear of the
Jews, Jesus came and stood among them and said, "Peace
be with you!" After he said this, he showed them his hands
and side. The disciples were overjoyed when they saw the
Lord.

Again Jesus said, "Peace be with you! *As the Father has
sent me, I am sending you.*" And with that he breathed on
them and said, "Receive the Holy Spirit. If you forgive anyone his sins, they are forgiven; if you do not forgive them,
they are not forgiven."

—John 20:19–23

Take note. Jesus allowed these followers—as he does us—only
a few seconds of unrestrained joy before he harnessed that joy
into ministry: "As the Father has sent me, I am sending you." As I
came to you, you must go to others. As I taught, you teach. As I
brought healing, you bring it to those you meet. As I sacrificed,
even unto death, so must you.

Jesus breathed the promised Holy Spirit upon them, empow-
ering them to do what they needed to do. They would understand
it all fully a few weeks later with the outpouring at Pentecost, but
Jesus had already told them how important their ministry was. If
they offered the message of forgiveness, people would accept it.
If they refused to pass the message along, it would not be received.
They had in their hands the power either to share the message
with the world or to let it die.

I'm so thankful that they shared the message. These very disciples used their different gifts to teach, preach, write, heal, lead,
correct, train, and do a host of other ministry tasks.

Today, the survival of the message is up to us. Just as the disciples' joy did for them, our joy, too, must translate—immediately—into ministry. We must teach, preach, heal, lead, correct,
train, and help. We must do whatever it is that God has called us

to do. We must discover our spiritual gifts and use them efficiently for the glory of God.

From pastor Tony Campolo comes the story of a young woman named Nancy. She came to the end of herself, and nearly to the end of her life when, intent on suicide, she jumped from the balcony of her apartment. Instead of dying, however, she awoke in a hospital room, paralyzed from the waist down.

In the midst of that pain, fear, and confusion, she turned to Christ. As she listened with her heart, she recounted the way that Jesus came to her and said very clearly, "You have had a healthy body and a crippled soul. From this day on, you will have a crippled body, but you will have a healthy soul."

Nancy said, "I gave my life to Jesus that night in that hospital room, and I knew that if I kept a healthy soul, it would mean that I would have to help other people. And so I do."

Her newfound joy led to ministry. Now she runs a weekly classified ad in the personals section of her local newspaper. Her ad reads, "If you are lonely or have a problem, call me. I am in a wheelchair, and I seldom get out. We can share our problems with each other. I'd love to talk."

As many as thirty people a week call Nancy, lightening their own loads of anxiety and discouragement and bringing a wonderful sense of meaning to Nancy's life.

How simple. She gave her life to Christ, and Jesus gave her a job. Her paycheck? She's been blessed, she said. She has a newfound peace and joy beyond comprehension.

You can't help believing that the Lord Jesus looks at a life that's been changed like that and smiles. It's easy to imagine a twinkle in his eye and a wonderful, heavenly sound echoing off the walls of heaven. Can you hear it?

It's laughter.

Imitate it.

Endnotes

Chapter 5: Laughing in the Face of Death

1. Taken from personal illustration files.

Chapter 7: An Offer of Peace

1. Jim Morris, "Tis the season—for burglaries: Tips for protecting your home," available http://www.CNN.com, 27 August 1999.

Chapter 8: Laughter Is a Battle

1. Charles Odum, "Warner makes unlikely jump from stock boy to NFL MVP," *Macon Telegraph*, 26 January 2000, 1C.

Chapter 9: "Come Now; Let Us Leave"

1. *New American Standard Bible* (La Habra, Calif.: Lockman Foundation, 1960, 1962, 1963, 1968, 1971, 1972, 1973, 1975, 1977).
2. *The Twentieth Century New Testament* (Old Tappan, N.J.: Revell, 1904).

3. George M. Lamsa, *Holy Bible from Ancient Eastern Manuscripts* (Philadelphia: A. J. Holman Co., 1957).

4. J. B. Phillips, *New Testament in Modern English* (New York: Macmillan, 1958).

Chapter 10: The Laughter of Bearing Fruit

1. "A Not-So-Simple Twist of Fate," *The American Funeral Director,* January 2000, 5.

Chapter 12: Laughter at a Funeral

1. Tracy Stewart, *Payne Stewart: The Authorized Biography* (Nashville: Broadman and Holman, 2000), 275.

Chapter 13: Never Alone

1. Taken from personal illustration files.

Chapter 15: The Laughter of a Champion

1. *The Bible in Basic English* (Cambridge: University Press, in association with Evans Brothers, 1949).

2. *The New English Bible* (The Delegates of the Oxford University Press and the Syndics of the Cambridge University Press, 1961, 1970). Reprinted by permission.

3. Helen Spurrell, *A Translation of the Old Testament Scriptures from the Original Hebrew* (London: James Nisbet, 1985).

4. Ronald Knox, *The New Testament in the Translation of Monsignor Ronald Knox* (New York: Sheed and Ward, 1944).

5. James A. R. Moffatt, *The Bible: James Moffatt Translation* (reprint, Grand Rapids: Kregel, 1994).

6. Joseph Bryant Rotherham, *The Emphasized Bible* (Grand Rapids: Kregel, 1994).

7. *New Jerusalem Bible* (Garden City: Doubleday, 1985).

8. *New Testament: A Translation in Language of the People* (Williams, 1937).

Also by Andy Cook

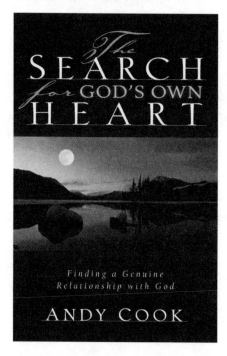

The Search for God's Own Heart

0-8254-2389-9
paperback

You *can* know the heart of God.

It's an intriguing idea, isn't it? Perhaps it's a new concept for you. Or perhaps, like so many people, the idea has captivated you but all your past attempts at developing a genuine relationship with God have only left you frustrated.

Andy Cook knows exactly how you feel, and he wants to take you on a compelling journey toward the heart of God through the story of King David. In *The Search for God's Own Heart* you will discover how to open your heart to God's signs, which are rarely flashing neon. Let the search begin!

"Easy to read, but . . . hard-hitting."
—*Church Libraries*